Restorative Communities

◆ ◆ ◆

From Conflict to Conversation

by
Kerra Bolton

THE PIPER'S PRESS
Pipersville, Pennsylvania • USA

RESTORATIVE COMMUNITIES:
FROM CONFLICT TO CONVERSATION

by Kerra Bolton

PRINT ISBN: 978-1-934355-61-9
EBOOK ISBN: 978-1-934355-62-6

FIRST EDITION

Published by
THE PIPER'S PRESS
P.O. Box 400
Pipersville, PA 18947 USA

DESIGNED BY
The Word Forge

VISIT OUR WEBSITE: BANR.FOUNDATION

Restorative Communities

◆◆◆

From Conflict to Conversation

Table of Contents

1

My Journey to
a New Reality

I came to Mexico to die.

I was broken, and in 2016 I broke up with America. I felt strangely orphaned in my forties, after the recent deaths of my parents. The well of romantic prospects dried up, and I wasn't willing to swipe right to find a new partner. So instead, I built a successful political communications consultancy, advising education and healthcare organizations about media and public policy, but the work was unfulfilling.

My friendships felt performative. We met for "Game Night" to see the latest superhero blockbuster or to have cocktails in the hottest new restaurants. But once the photos were snapped and posted to social media, there was no substance, depth, or meaning in our interactions.

Also, I lost faith in my country. As a Black woman, I have always known the truth about America. The United States is a country that has aspired, especially after World War II, to be a beacon of democracy throughout the world. However, its "freedom" was built on the whip lashes on the backs of my ancestors, the tears of Native American tribes, the internment of Japanese Americans, and the subjugation of LGBTQ+ people.

Nevertheless, I always believed the arc of social justice leaned upward. I thought that if I did my part—graduate from college, speak "proper" English, demonstrate in my dress and comportment that I was not a threat, that I was "just like" white people—white people would do their part. Mainly, I hoped white people would "allow" blacks to enjoy the same fruits of freedom at best, or at the very least, leave us alone.

"White Faust" never honored their end of the bargain like I foolishly thought they would. The white people in question were not the Confederate flag-waving, functionally illiterate racists lampooned in popular culture. Instead, the white people who broke my heart were the supposed "good ones"—the ones with whom I rode the bus to integrated schools, invited to my home for dinner, worked alongside toward shared ideals.

Many white people I knew doubled down on their apathy and cowardice during the summer of 2016, in the wake of several deaths of unarmed Black men at the hands of white police officers. The deaths of Philando Castile and Alton Sterling awakened my sense of racial justice like no other incident before, and unlocked a personal tragedy I hid for 25 years. There were videos of the police killing Castile and Sterling in both cases, and the "good" white people I hoped would call for police reform retreated into silence.

There was no place for me to express my justifiable rage at the injustices. My uncle died of cancer in April 2016, and my mother wasn't far behind. She was battling stomach cancer after surviving Non-Hodgkin's Lymphoma and breast cancer. Mom died in August 2016.

The "nice" white people withdrew, and my Black friends were dealing with their own trauma. America burrowed deeper into roots of white supremacism, willful ignorance, greed; and homophobia blossomed after the election of President Donald Trump. But I was living in Mexico by then.

Life allowed me to rest, but not to die. I had lived in a small beach community in the Mexican Caribbean for nearly two years, when I received a phone call in January 2018 from Ted Wachtel, a restorative practices pioneer.

Billed as the "science of relationships," restorative practices are a series of protocols ranging from affective questions to formal conferences seeking to repair harm, restore relationships, and build social capital. Restorative practices operate from the underlying premise that people tend to be happier, more productive, and likelier to make positive changes when those in authority do things with them, rather than to or for them.

Ted read an article I wrote for CNN.com, "How Black Women Saved Alabama and Democracy." He appreciated my skepticism and professional expertise as a former political journalist, operative, and consultant. Ted asked if I would be interested in collaborating with an organization, Building a New Reality (BANR), which he co-founded with his wife, Susan. At the time, BANR was defined as a "non-partisan, evidence-based social movement that explores models of decentralized power and participatory decision-making, including restorative practices, to address society's broad needs— governance, learning, justice, care, spirit, and enterprise."

Over the next four years, Ted and Susan created a series of opportunities that spanned the globe and allowed me to observe experiments in building a new reality. I learned about restorative practices through reading research and case studies, witnessing their practical application in Detroit, and participating in a hands-on workshop at the International Institute for Restorative Practices (IIRP). Founded by Ted and Susan, IIRP is the world's first accredited graduate school wholly devoted to restorative practices.

Along the way, I attended a daylong neighborhood summit in which police officers and the citizens they serve learned what it takes to keep communities safe from the other group's point of view. In addition, university professors met with me to explain their cutting-edge research on restorative practices in local prisons to reduce recidivism rates.

District court employees also shared stories about how they employed restorative practices to de-escalate conflicts in the workplace that previously left dried spit on both sides of the customer service window. A 15-year-old black male in Detroit said using restorative practices at school and in his neighborhood helped him and his friends pause before reaching for a gun.

Each experience with restorative practices cracked me open a little more. If a self-described "old school" principal can change his ways, so can I. My willingness to be open to restorative practices begged a question: Could restorative practices help heal the broken relationships I ran away from when I moved to Mexico?

Answering that question led to my role producing and participating in the award-winning docuseries, *Detroit Rising: How The Motor City Becomes A Restorative City* and *Finding Hope*, a documentary short film, with Cassidy Friedman, a San Francisco-based filmmaker. *Detroit Rising* followed me as I engaged with Black grassroots leaders who implemented restorative practices in nearly every sector of the city. *Finding Hope* spotlighted a community of care that enveloped a teenage girl struggling with low self-esteem during a drug relapse at CSF/Buxmont, a youth treatment center in rural Pennsylvania.

This book, *Restorative Communities: From Conflict to Conversation*, is a culmination of my four-year journey. It is a collection of unpublished essays and blog posts written for the BANR website (buildinganewreality.com). Each section of the book addresses a specific societal need. In addition, restorative practices pioneers have also contributed several essays to this book, and are highlighted for the reader.

Two audiences inspired the writing of this book. First are readers who are working in the area of restorative practices. They have attended classes, workshops, and may even have studied at IIRP. These readers struggle with translating classroom curricula to their daily experiences. The second set of readers have vaguely heard about restorative practices. They aren't interested in the academic aspects of restorative practices, but they want to strengthen relationships in their family, workplace, and community. Even if you are somewhere in between, that's okay. *Restorative Communities* is still for you.

I hope my story and the others presented in *Restorative Communities* inspire meaningful conversations and concrete actions around what it takes to build a new reality. In our fractured ways, we are all looking for a sense of belonging, a path to make critical decisions, and a process to resolve conflicts. May we not only restore our communities; but our faith in ourselves, each other, and the future.

2

Defining a Restorative Community

What is a restorative community?

It is easier to define a restorative community by what it isn't. A restorative community is not characterized by size or the diversity of its population. It isn't gentrification. We don't measure its success by low unemployment, the number of greenways winding through concrete streets, high test scores in public schools, or even an index of factors that encompass a general definition of "quality of life."

The simplest definition of a restorative community is a place where restorative practices permeate the six facets of societal need, as identified by Ted Wachtel's "Building a New Reality" framework. Each facet—Governance, Learning, Spirit, Care, Justice, and Enterprise—represents a broad category of society's needs. The remainder of this book is organized around the themes of the societal facets.

Ted explains, "The six facets provide a roadmap to where we've been and where we may want to go. They also represent a framework for action that defines the dimensions of a non-partisan, evidence-based social movement that mobilizes and inspires us to improve the quality and civility of conversation and decision-making throughout society by fostering more voice, choice, and shared responsibility."

Imagine a place where municipal court staff comes together to calmly address employee conflicts before those staff members interface with the general public who arrive at the courthouse doors on what could be the worst day of their lives.

What about a place where workers burn their annual employment contract at the end of the year as a symbolic reminder that their work is more than a paycheck? Employees still retain their legal protections. However, their employment is not legally defined as "at will," but instead becomes a daily decision to devote one's time and talents to achieve an organizational mission.

Or what if your child attended a school where parents, teachers, and community members were co-creators of a rich learning environment where the student guides the educational process?

Decentralized Power and Participatory Decision-Making

Skeptics often respond to the abovementioned scenarios by insisting that they don't exist in the "real world."

Restorative communities aren't the stuff of fairytales. Nevertheless, they exist in places like Detroit and Kortrijk, Belgium. Moreover, when communities are rooted in restorative practices, residents experience better customer service, a more positive experience of local government, and an increase in academic attainment by their children.

"At the heart of every facet of the New Reality," Ted says, "is decentralized power and participatory decision-making."

The idea of decentralized power and participatory decision-making sounds scary to people for whom structure and hierarchy are synonymous with a fair and just society because it sounds like no one is "in charge." To whom do we complain to fix the potholes on public roads, for example? Who will decide how to spend billions of dollars of taxpayer money for state government programs and services? "We can't all decide," critics might think. Others might oppose decentralized power and participatory decision-making because they believe that if they do so, it will mean surrendering power and control they have not earned yet enjoyed. Decentralized power and participatory decision-making are the essences of true democracy and representation. However, instituting them doesn't result in an environment in which no one is in charge. On the contrary, everyone shares a responsibility to and accountability for common agreed-upon values.

Characteristics of Restorative Communities

We'll see real-world examples of decentralized power and participatory decision-making in later chapters of this book.

I believe that creating a sense of belonging, providing a pathway to making decisions, and offering a sound process to resolve conflicts are vital to the success of a restorative community. Restorative communities also share two or more of the following characteristics:

> Decentralized power and participatory decision-making are sewn in the fabric of organizational or community culture. It's how they "do" things.

> Restorative Practices are adopted in at least three of the six facets of societal needs—Learning, Governance, Care, Justice, Enterprise, and Spirit.

> Implementing restorative practices comes from the community. It isn't a government program subject to annual budgets and political whim.

> Restorative practices are cross-pollinated throughout the community. For example, police departments use restorative practices to engage the community, even in schools and neighborhoods where restorative practices are embedded.

› There are regular and frequent opportunities to learn about or strengthen one's restorative practices knowledge through workshops and classes.

Does Geography Shape Destiny?

Employing this framework to define a restorative city led me to explore the enactment of restorative practices in two different cities halfway across the world—Detroit, Michigan, and Kortrijk, Belgium. Specifically, I examined experimental models in both cities that addressed at-risk communities and the workplace. Family and work are ripe for exploration because that's where we spend the most time and where we are most invested. What percentage of your conversations with friends and family is about misunderstandings at work and family issues? Family and work are also where interpersonal power is expressed and sometimes abused. Therefore, they offer the most significant opportunities for healing.

I also believe that geography shapes destiny.

This is not to say that where we are born should determine our educational attainment, the trajectory of our careers, and who we can and should love. However, I believe that our lives are shaped by the way a magnolia tree at the local park dips in the surface of the water, the corner convenience store that always stocks our favorite brand of potato chips, or the lone strength of a stone church in a neighborhood pockmarked by abandoned homes. Such landmarks touch the interior geography of our soul and serve as a common rallying point for our shared civic aspirations.

Detroit and Kortrijk have distinct geographies and demographics that have shaped their destiny. However, their unique and distinctive approaches to implementing restorative practices in their cities offer lessons on the nature of empowerment, responsibility, home, family, and community.

The Motor City

Detroit is a fertile ground to become America's first true "Restorative City" because of its rich yet troubled history, population trends, diverse culture, location, and economic importance in the regional and national economies. Nearly 80 percent of Detroit's population is comprised of African Americans, according to the latest U.S. Census data available. Whether in Detroit or elsewhere in the United States, Black Americans have endured a long and painful history as a population to whom things are done, not necessarily for or with.

Alice Thompson, Henry McClendon, Commander Eric Ewing, and others, whom we'll meet later in this book, are among a group of community leaders whose influence spans the city's diverse ethnic enclaves, whose networks are creating lasting change. They are initiating and implementing a quiet revolution, through which restorative practices give Black children the confidence to believe their voice matters. Residents become co-creators with the police to keep their communities safe, and neighborhoods become safe havens for children and families.

I will take you behind the scenes of a daylong neighborhood summit, in which police officers and the citizens they serve learned what it takes to keep communities safe. In addition, District court employees share their stories about resolving conflicts in the workplace that previously left dried spit on both sides of the customer window.

An Old-World Soul

Kortrijk, Belgium, is half a world away from Detroit—especially in geography, population, and economics.

Located in West Flanders, Kortrijk is a three-hour train ride from Paris and Amsterdam. It is a modern city with an "Old World" soul. Cars and bicycles race along winding roads. Global retailers such as H&M and Zara perch beside traditional chocolatiers and waffle shops in the city's bustling downtown shopping center. Kortrijk's long association with the flax trade has made it one of the wealthiest cities in the region. However, beneath the polish of Kortrijk's chic restaurants, the thriving arts community and ancient glamour of medieval architecture are families in crisis. We'll explore this phenomenon later in this book.

Nevertheless, nonprofit leaders are partnering with city officials to implement restorative practices to programs, services, and public spaces that help troubled youths and their families.

Unlike most restorative practices techniques—which often take place in conference rooms and offices—Belgians incorporate nature and movement. We'll see more examples of this innovative approach in subsequent chapters.

In addition, curiosity and openness govern tough, ethical inquiries and lead to better solutions for the staff of a social service organization grappling with burnout amidst an ever-growing roster of responsibilities. We'll look at how restorative practices guided that organization through a management crisis that flattened its leadership for the better.

When terrorist attacks in Brussels rocked the nation in 2016, circles—the most basic form of restorative practices—facilitated community healing. Likewise, restorative practices form the bedrock to aid the influx of refugee children and youth who fled atrocities no child should witness.

Why Detroit and Kortrijk

Other cities around the world, such as Leeds and Hull in the United Kingdom, are making strides to become restorative cities or at the very least incorporate restorative practices in their public schools.

Those efforts are to be applauded. I chose Detroit and Kortrijk because each city illustrates the creative possibilities of restorative practices to address the urgent issues of our time. These wildly contrasting cities challenge assumptions about race, economic status, and political ideology. Finally, I chose them because the prime movers in Detroit and Kortrijk are not government agencies, but nonprofit, community-based organizations.

Restorative practices aren't just for "urban" centers grappling with crime, poverty, violence, and unemployment. Nor are they only successful in suburban, white communities with some institutional support. Building a restorative city is possible anywhere—regardless of demographics, geography, and politics— because anything is possible when residents with restorative hearts gather and commit themselves to a common purpose.

3

Learning

We confuse learning with school, according to Ted, who began his education career in the classroom and later founded successful learning models that have served "at risk" youth since 1977.

Learning is misconstrued as "measured by the number of years spent in school and the number of diplomas collected." That's schooling. Learning, formal or informal, is "acquired through direct experience, and self-directed learning, driven by personal interest." It's usually regarded as less worthy than schooling.

However, the global pandemic challenged traditional notions of schooling and learning. By removing the classroom, creative opportunities opened in the way children learn, achieve academic benchmarks, and interact with their peers.

In a restorative community, "freedom of learning will soon stand alongside freedom of religion—fully recognized as a basic human right."

The following essays explore non-traditional approaches to learning based on restorative practices. Some approaches use the traditional classroom setting as a base while using restorative practices to create a dynamic and interactive academic culture.

Restorative Practices Give Hope
to Hope Academy Charter School

Dr. Ronald Williams, then superintendent of Hope Academy Charter School in Detroit, is a self-described "old school educator" who spent most of his 30 years as a strict disciplinarian.

"Before, when students had problems, we suspended them and sent them home," he said. "But that's not a punishment because they wind up watching TV and playing video games while their parents work."

The continued prevalence and impact of the disproportionate rate at which black students are suspended and expelled from school are well-documented. I uncovered dozens of personal stories behind the statistics. I was an education policy journalist, a strategic communications consultant, and a lobbyist for a statewide school choice organization. I also worked as the nonprofit's executive director, which helped transformational Black educators and community leaders develop and maintain charter schools.

Hope Academy in Detroit was like many schools I advised in recent years. It was founded, in part, to counteract these trends and stem the tide of academic and social disparities Black children in Detroit experienced. The school is family-oriented, and much of its staff has been employed at the school since its inception.

While the school has enjoyed academic success and broad community support, school leaders turned to learning about and then implementing restorative practices to change the culture of its classrooms and maybe even the surrounding community. Integrating restorative practices in its school culture was the next practical step in evolving a healthy classroom climate that put the children's needs first.

Hope Academy Takes a Restorative Approach

In a sun-dappled room at Hope Academy, I interviewed Dr. Williams, Principal Patricia Davis, and Keisha Allen. At the time,

Keisha served as Hope Academy's program director and was known as a top restorative practices trainer.

The room, Keisha told me, symbolized the school's ongoing commitment to implementing restorative practices. Perched on a rug is a group of chairs pre-arranged in a large, open circle. A desk for a teacher or school administrator is nestled in the corner. But the real action seems to happen in the circle—in the held space where issues are discussed, trust is earned, and wounds have the potential to be healed.

"This room was designed and created by the young people," Keisha said. "We wanted the young people to have a voice in how this space looked and would be used."

Hope Academy school leaders have adopted a restorative approach. Administrators believe students, teachers, and staff are happier and more likely to make positive changes when authority figures do things with them, rather than to them or for them. As a result, they use restorative practices in nearly every aspect of the school's operations.

Student suspensions plummeted from 113 to 7 between the 2016-2017 and 2017-2018 school years. School administrators credit asking students the five restorative questions when responding to challenging behavior and the regular use of proactive and reactive restorative circles. Restorative questions include:

> What happened?
> What were you thinking at the time?
> What have you thought about since?
> Who has been affected by what you have done and in what way?
> What do you think you need to do to make things right?

The questions are part of Ted's book, *Restorative Circles in Schools: Building Community and Enhancing Learning,* but they originated with Australian restorative pioneer Terry O'Connell. Ted states: "These questions separate people's behavior from their intrinsic worth as a person, allowing them to admit their mistakes, right their wrongs, and be reintegrated into a community."

Restorative circles, Ted explains, "enable students and a teacher or other school leaders to meet to discuss, answer questions, solve problems, play a game, or offer feedback. Circles have structure, purpose, and focus, and can be personal, academic, or work-related."

Principal Davis called restorative circles the "noise killer" because it gives teachers clear, actionable feedback. A restorative circle was convened at Hope Academy, for example, when a teacher didn't understand why she wasn't getting expected results from students despite her best efforts. Students said they liked the teacher, but she didn't allow them to express themselves. Consequently, the teacher learned that before she could educate her students, she must first build relationships with them.

"Integrating restorative practices in an educational setting is a process," said Davis. "People have to be willing to be changed, to have an open mind and an open heart."

Changing Classrooms, Changing Communities

One of the hurdles of implementing restorative practices in a school setting is mitigating students' conflicting messages at home and in their communities.

Family and community members might pressure children to respond to conflicts with violence to defend themselves. However, restorative practices enable children to hear a different message from responsible adults, who encourage compromise and working together.

For example, when two boys were fighting in the hallway, Dr. Williams said he pulled the boys aside, took them to his office, and performed a restorative circle. As a result, the boys were friends again when they left his office and planned to repair the harm to others that their fight had caused.

Through restorative practices, the approach to conflict at Hope Academy has changed from punishing to promising. "Restorative practices helped me to look at myself and learn to be less punitive, listen more, and exercise patience," Dr. Williams said. "Going forward, when I make decisions, they will be in the best interests of the students, and they will be restorative."

Interviewing school administrators at Hope Academy gave me hope because I watched ordinary people work to examine themselves and their actions with courage, intelligence, and humility. Through restorative practices, students gain opportunities to be co-creators of their classrooms. Teachers strive to develop an educational environment that works for the students as much as it works for them. And an old-school educator like Dr. Williams can become reborn in his beloved profession.

Hope Academy and
the Power of Student Voices

The scrape of metal desks against the floor signaled the start of a restorative circle at Hope Academy Charter School in Detroit. Selected to be "Restorative Practices Ambassadors," a group of eighth graders met once a month with Assistant Principal Rhonda Calloway, to communicate the concerns and interests of their peers to school staff and administrators.

Rhonda calmed the turbulence of emotions swirling in and among the students, to focus on the task by establishing questions like, "If you could describe your feelings right now as a season, what would you be?"

Students passed a spongy ball when it was their turn to speak. Rhonda adjusted the tuning fork of her listening skills. She knew when to ask the student a follow-up question, when to pull back, and when to ask the group for advice in dealing with their peer's situation.

"How are you incorporating restorative practices in your home, community, and school?" Rhonda leaned in.

Most students' answers were about helping others solve problems or intervening at the verge of an argument. Restorative Practices Ambassadors also served as peer mentors, especially when it came to conflict resolution and prompting conversations that promoted deeper thinking, reflection, and accountability. The ambassadors weren't necessarily the best students or star athletes, though some were.

Blaise Armstead was one of those students. Handsome, charismatic, and intelligent, he communicated wisdom beyond his years and the charm of a young person whose quick wit and smile are often called upon to ease social situations.

"I was at football practice, and I hit someone a little too hard,"Blaise said. "He said, 'I feel disrespected,' and I said, "What can I do to make it better?"

A Stolen Childhood

Leading with curiosity and asking restorative questions such as "what can I do to make it better?" de-escalate the potential for violence.

School violence disproportionately affects Black children compared to their classmates. Waves of national research in 2018 found that Black students in K-12 schools throughout the United States are more likely to be disproportionately suspended, expelled, and referred to law enforcement no matter the type of school or level of poverty rate among students.

According to a federal civil rights investigation, Black students are punished more harshly than their white classmates, even when they engage in identical or similar behavior.

The National Center for Learning Disabilities found that Black students with disabilities are almost three times as likely to experience out-of-school suspension or expulsion as their white peers.

In addition, Black girls are six times as likely to be suspended as white girls. In contrast, Black boys are three times as likely to be suspended as white boys, according to research from Columbia Law School's Center for Intersectionality and Social Policy Studies.

Suspending and expelling students can negatively affect student achievement and increase students' risk of dropping out and their likelihood of future involvement with the criminal justice system, according to a report by the Education Commission of the States, a nonprofit education policy think tank.

Helping Students Find Their Voice

Restorative practices enable Black youth, among the most vulnerable, economically disenfranchised, and criminalized at increasingly early ages, to find, express, and develop their unique voice.

"I was raised in a way that said men are supposed to mask their feelings because it's considered feminine if you cry," Blaise said. "I'm not the only one who shares their feelings in a circle. With restorative practices, there is another option. But there's a little mushiness to it, and I'm still getting used to it."

However, it's precisely by teaching young people how to wade through their intense feelings rather than ignore emotions as an impediment to learning that sets Hope Academy apart from other schools that incorporate a more traditional approach. Emotions, school staff and administrators believe, are transmitters of deeper truths whose hidden wisdom is as vital as learning grammatical structure or calculating algebra formulas.

Every Teacher Is a Safe Haven

Awkward, shy, intelligent, and passionate about writing, Nyla approached Rhonda after the circle and asked to meet with the educator after school.

Unlike Blaise, whose charisma shone a natural spotlight on him wherever he went, Nyla didn't stand out among her peers. She was quiet and observant. Her presence was like a gentle stream carving a path among the rocks. Nyla had a disagreement with her friends before the circle and wanted advice from Rhonda on how to handle it.

"I like that they know me," Rhonda said after the students emptied out of the classroom. "They know that they are important to me, that they fit. When they don't fit, they want a circle. Every student knows that every teacher is a haven."

Rhonda and Nyla met in an empty classroom after school. Nyla's moon-shaped face had shadows of worry crossing over it. Nyla explained in a sweet, soft voice that her friends said they don't confide in her because she's sensitive and cries a lot.

Swaying from side to side, Nyla talked as if she could barely contain the swirl of emotions. She said, "It makes me so sad that no one can talk to me because they are afraid of hurting my feelings. I know that I'm sensitive, but it's not their decision not to talk to me in a real way."

Rhonda listened attentively and asked clarifying questions to get to the heart of the matter.

"Have you expressed your feelings to them?" Rhonda asked.

"They say they can't talk to me," Nyla said.

"Why do you think they can't?"

"Because I cry."

"There's nothing wrong with crying," Rhonda said. "A mini-baptism clears the soul. Do you think we need to call a circle?"

Nyla declined the offer. She didn't want her friends to know that she talked to Rhonda about it. Nyla decided the solution was to "toughen up."

"Ask yourself, 'when these feelings occur, how does it make you feel?'" Rhonda counseled. "Until we get in touch with these feelings, we're not going to be able to get to the root of the problem. I'm glad you felt like it was okay to open up to me, because this wouldn't have happened last year."

Rhonda and Nyla stood up and hugged. Relief washed across Nyla's face. Unfortunately, Rhonda didn't solve Nyla's problems. But Nyla had a path forward, and that was enough for now.

The Power of Small, Ordinary Moments

There was nothing life-threatening about Nyla's situation.

It was a typical teenage problem that might loom large for a few days and fade before the next emotional act begins. But that's precisely the point.

When chronicling the lives of ordinary people in a dense, urban landscape like Detroit, observers often go for the most dramatic narratives. They highlight the mother seeking justice after the death of her teenage son in a drive-by shooting, a conflict between tenants and a landlord about much-needed repairs, or rival gangs engaged in a war that no one understands but the death toll mounts.

When applied thoughtfully and appropriately in these situations, restorative practices can repair harm, restore relationships, and build social capital. However, in the small, ordinary moments mentioned above between Nyla and Rhonda, restorative practices can be the most powerful. Transformation can happen one conversation at a time.

Tears fell down Rhonda's face soon after Nyla left the classroom. "When we first started implementing restorative practices," Rhonda said, "these students [including Nyla] were in the fifth and sixth grades." Rhonda continues, "Everyone kept passing and didn't want to talk. But today, she [Nyla] came to me. She came to me, and that's why it's [restorative practices] so good."

Restorative practices like circles are not only about solving conflicts. When used proactively, people can deploy circles to create a culture of openness and inclusion. Therefore, the inevitable conflicts can be resolved when they occur while preserving relationship bonds. Restorative practices in school settings allow students to learn their voice's power, potency, and dignity. Students understand through the actions and words of the adults in their learning environment that their lives matter.

Restorative practices also remove the power dynamic in which those in authority—teachers, city council members, police officers, or business leaders—decide whose life matters and whose doesn't. In the new reality, Detroit is building through restorative practices. Everyone's life matters because every voice matters.

"Whenever your voice is heard, you can always change the outcome," said Alice Thompson, former CEO of Black Family Education Services, which manages Hope Academy. "Our goal is to help those young people discover their gifts and talents. They can be Restorative Practices Ambassadors and presenters. Our young folks are on fire to do that type of work."

Hey, Black Child

I caught up with Nyla, Blaise, and the other students from Rhonda's circle at a city-wide event for student "Restorative Ambassadors," to share what they've learned.

Nyla was all smiles, and it seemed that some of the previous tension melted. She said she was trying to balance being a sensitive person with her friends' critical feedback. Next, Blaise and a female classmate took the stage to perform a spoken-word piece they had crafted.

"Hey, black child, do you know that you're strong?" Blaise asked the crowd. "Do you know your nation can be what you want it to be?"

"You can learn what you want to learn if you try to learn what you want to learn," the female classmate chimed in, matching Blaise's intensity.

"Be what you can be," they shouted in unison.

"Learn what you must learn," the girl said. "Do what you must do."

"So tomorrow, your nation will be what you want it to be," they exclaimed.

The crowd erupted in applause. Detroit's next generation of restorative leaders has spoken.

Igniting a New Reality in Public Education

It was the toughest crowd I had faced so far.

The middle-schoolers looked at me expectantly as I fumbled with the laptop. I was touring T'vier Secondary School in Kortrijk, Belgium, while exploring grassroots efforts to build a new reality by adapting restorative practices to meet the community's unique and urgent needs.

Founded in 2015 by a group of local parents, T'vier is an experiential school that bakes restorative practices into its culture, curricula, and pedagogy. The school models a "new reality" because students, teachers, parents, and community members form a collective educational experience.

Children learn better when the adults in their lives provide an academic environment in which students can co-create learning experiences and milestones that work best for them.

The school's pedological approach is based on "three pillars"—experience, investigation, and cooperation.

"T'vier is a dialect word that stands for 'fire,'" said An Algoed, one of the school's three care coordinators. "To teach is to ignite knowledge so that you are enthusiastic and on fire."

Experiential Education

The curricula are based on research and studies of what works in schools.

Lessons follow the Catholic school education curricula, enabling the school to be innovative while adhering to Flemish academic standards. Courses such as mathematics, Dutch, French, English, and Latin are self-paced.

Students who need focused and one-on-one instruction get it. The other students continue to practice the subject matter during independent study hours. In addition, educators evaluate students throughout the learning process to make sure they master the material.

Accountability is integrated into the curricula by allowing students to evaluate their progress through the "Rock, Paper, Scissors" method. Rock means that a student is progressing at an average pace. Paper means that the lesson is easy. Scissors denote that the student has difficulty mastering a lesson and may need extra help. In addition, each student is paired with a counselor who follows the student for two years. The counselor is responsible for the student's learning trajectory, works with the student individually or in class, and serves as the parent liaison. Competencies such as planning and studying, and social and emotional skills are also integrated into the school's curricula.

"It's more than hands-on learning," said Astrid, a T'vier student. "Usually, the teacher writes on the blackboard. Here, I can choose what I do and learn for myself."

Investigative Learning

The investigative aspect of T'vier comes as students are encouraged to research questions and apply what they learn to achieve their creative and academic edge.

School days are broken into circles, planning moments, independent working hours, quiet hours, instruction moments, a forum, and a project week. Students can work on their lessons during independent work hours with some guidance from teachers.

Educators don't teach subjects in silos. Instead, they bundle the natural sciences, engineering, history, geography, and the arts, as "projects." Religion and physical education are also offered. Students spend six weeks acquiring the basic knowledge of the subject and then applying what they learn to a project on which they work individually or in a group.

"I like that we're in small groups because you can connect with more people," said Liza, a T'vier student. "You can get to know more people."

Students present their projects at the end of six weeks to parents and the larger community. The presentations allow students to practice presentation and social development skills while showcasing the student's work.

Cooperative Community

As a cooperative school, educators believe in treating all members of their learning community equally.

They prioritize dialogue and consultation. Students are viewed as vessels of opportunity and possibility, not problems to be solved.

"We work together—teachers, parents, and pupils," said An, who also supervises the school's care coordinators. "We talk a lot on the phone. We are building this school together."

Circles are an integral tool for learning and community building. Educators introduce students to the circle concept early. Circles are also used to begin the day.

"If you have a circle, you bond with the teacher and your coach," Astrid said. "If something happens, it's easier to talk with them."

Parental participation is required. However, parents can choose their participation level, such as leading a workshop or becoming a member of the school's board. In addition, T'vier involves parents and other community members to participate in the students' education through its Friday workshops, which they call "studios." Neighborhood members are invited to give workshops on music, languages, technology, and other creative skills to supplement the curricula while truly involving the village to educate the child.

Expanding the Village

Here's where I come in.

Other than my Americanness, I wasn't much different from the other adults who add their verse to the academic conversation in which T'vier engages its students, parents, faculty, and the local community. But I wanted the T'vier students to understand that while their school differs from traditional, Flemish schools, they were connected to a larger, global community of students experiencing new ways of learning, connecting, communicating, and participating as responsible and active citizens.

I'm not sure if the Dutch students caught the American nuances. But I hope they saw a reflection of themselves and the possibility of what a new reality might bring—one in which our differences matter less than our shared humanity.

Many educators come to restorative practices to improve academic outcomes, build nourishing student relationships, reduce suspensions and expulsions, or cultivate an affirming school environment.

Used creatively, restorative practices can help schools build a bridge to other facets of societal needs. For example, in the following section, Adam Cronkright, an innovative champion of building a better democracy, used restorative practices to reshape student government elections while teaching students about the personal and collective benefits of participatory learning and decision-making.—KB

Democracy in Practice
By Adam Cronkright

Imagine a world in which schools didn't teach math.

Students interested in learning algebra or trigonometry could only do so in an after-school math club. And imagine that each school's math club was reserved for a few popular and high-achieving students, no one else.

Fortunately, we don't live in that world. So, although not every student receives the same support or reaches the same level, each has the right to a basic foundation and the opportunity to advance in math, as in other important subjects like science, art, and language—popularity be damned.

But what about civic and leadership education? Schools may teach students about the three branches of government, but few provide courses specifically to develop civic and leadership skills. For example, how many of us left high school and can effectively facilitate a meeting?

The only formal tool for hands-on learning in this domain is typically an extracurricular club called "student government" or "student council." And because student governments are formed through competitive school-wide elections, they usually comprise a few popular and high-achieving students, no one else.

Our organization, Democracy In Practice, is changing this. We are a nonprofit dedicated to democratic innovation in educational contexts. For the past six years, we have helped schools in Bolivia take three major steps to transform student government. We started our work in Bolivia because one of our co-founders is from there. Still, the changes I share here could make student government a richer and more inclusive educational experience across the globe.

Lotteries: From Popularity to Probability

The first and most important step in reinventing student government has been replacing competitive elections with voluntary lotteries.

Lotteries give all interested students an equal chance (probability) to become a representative and develop civic and leadership skills—popularity be damned. Moreover, because lotteries don't disadvantage shyer and less popular students, they form student governments that are far more diverse and representative than those formed through elections.

Not only are lotteries fairer and more inclusive, but they are also more fun. Each participant experiences a moment when they could win, and their excitement isn't tainted by questions of popularity and fear of rejection. So, it's not surprising that the students and teachers in these schools have preferred lotteries to the old popularity contests.

Using lotteries to select representatives is not new. Over 2,000 years ago, Athenian citizens used lotteries to fill most public offices. Today, lotteries are being used worldwide to form citizens assemblies that weigh in on important policy decisions. Democracy in Practice appears to be the first organization to use this ancient, democratic practice to select student representatives. We'll explore some surprising implications of this innovative use [later in this chapter].

Rotation to Increase Participation

After lotteries, the second step toward transforming student government has been introducing various forms of rotation.

We eliminated the traditional position of president and rotated responsibilities so that every student representative learns to set agendas, facilitate meetings, and speak in front of the school.

Additionally, we shortened their term lengths from a full school year to a semester. This rotation of office is inspired by the regular rotation of leadership in the traditional ayllu system of government, which is still practiced in many indigenous Bolivian communities. The shorter terms give more students a chance to participate in student government while still affording them enough time to have a rich and memorable experience.

Empowerment and Encouragement

The third and final step in this transformation has been empowering student governments.

We provide extensive capacity building and educator support, such as facilitation training, public speaking workshops, and help with project management. We also encourage student representatives to go beyond the typical task of organizing a school dance and work on their chosen real and consequential initiatives.

As a result, we've seen them acquire recycling bins and first aid kits for their schools, undertake reforestation projects and even open a library. They've cut student transportation costs, organized and financed school-wide trips to museums and botanical gardens, and pressured local authorities to make school repairs and improve school lunches.

In the process, they've met directly with principles, PTAs, district directors, police, nonprofits, mayors, and even the Minister of Education. This experience builds their social skills, self-esteem, and familiarity with the school and local government. These are three simple but important steps.

Lotteries open student government to everyone, rotation increases participation, and proper support empowers students to tackle real issues they care about. At least in these schools, just as every student has an opportunity to learn and excel in math, every student has a chance to develop civic skills and become a leader. Now imagine a world that's true for every student in every school.

Lotteries, Leadership and Biases

Our approach has centered on replacing competitive elections with voluntary lotteries. This gives every student, even those lacking the charisma and popularity to win an election, an equal chance to become a student representative and develop civic and leadership skills.

When we first started replacing elections, we did it because we felt every student deserves an equal chance to develop civic and leadership skills. We figured that the "unelectable" students, who were finally given an opportunity through the lotteries, would need more support. Likewise, we assumed that the few charismatic high achievers selected in the lotteries would require less of our attention and provide critical leadership for their peers. But for the most part, our experience has been the opposite.

Changing the Perception of Leadership

Lotteries change the perception of student government from being rooted in popularity to being rooted in equality.

In our work, we found that critical leadership has regularly come from students who struggle with homework, making friends, or speaking in public. They worry us at first but prove us wrong by showing up for meetings, listening to their teammates, and following through with the things they say they will do.

Conversely, often our greatest challenge is with students who are at the top of their class, popular, and charismatic. They make great first impressions but then start showing up late or skipping meetings, try to dominate conversations, and don't follow through on their commitments. Sometimes they even attempt to hog the credit for their team's achievements.

Now, obviously, not every popular kid is a terrible teammate, and not every shy student becomes a standout. It is also true that confidence and charisma are important aspects of leadership. But especially in democratic settings, leadership requires many other important traits and comes in many diverse forms. For example, we've found it much easier to teach respectful and reliable teammates to overcome their fear of public speaking than to teach students who talk the talk to set aside their egos, work well with others, and walk the walk.

Yet, in our assessment of leadership potential, we are continuously fooled by the presence (or lack) of confidence, charisma, and credentials (which in a school setting amount to academic or athletic achievement). I have heard teachers sing the praises of a student they saw as a "leader," unaware that the student was on the verge of being voted out of the student government.

The reverse can also be true, as the story of a student whom I'll call José will illustrate.

When José was selected in the lottery, a teacher warned me that he was a "bad student" who was repeating the eighth grade and would "not work out." However, a semester later, José received special recognition for going above and beyond during his term of office.

We can't take credit for any magical transformation. Truth is, he still struggled in the classroom. But to everyone's surprise (including ours), he showed other important interests and qualities that he had never been given a chance to discover, develop, and demonstrate.

Unlearning Leadership Biases

Elections channel and reinforce our narrow and superficial leadership biases.

Only students with competitive ambition, charisma, and popularity tend to win elections and get labeled as "leaders." Therefore, young people learn that those are the key characteristics needed to be a leader. But, when we look at the state of adult politics, is this really what we want to be teaching the next generation?

I used to think that elections were unfair because they favor the most promising student leaders and rob all others of the opportunity to develop skills they desperately lack. I still believe every young person should have the opportunity. However, having worked closely with hundreds of student representatives selected in both lotteries and elections, I've realized that I was wrong in my assessment of promise and lack.

The truth is elections advantage and often select students with the least leadership potential and close the door to students with the most. Fortunately, lotteries provide a simple and fair way to sidestep our deeply ingrained leadership biases and give students the opportunity to surprise us all.

The Benefits of Student Lotteries

Unlike elections, lotteries don't discriminate.

They don't care about charisma or popularity, and they don't respect cliques. As such, student governments selected by lottery are far more diverse and representative of the student population than those that are elected. Moreover, we structure the lotteries to ensure an even gender balance and a representation of different grade levels and classrooms.

In our work, the typical student government has six girls and six guys, ranging from 12 to 18 years of age. They have various traits, talents, personalities, interests, home lives, and grade point averages. There is almost always among their ranks a skilled athlete or two, a dancer, a musician, a voracious reader, a budding artist, and an avid gamer.

Fast Friends

It always amazes us how quickly these very different students, who would not typically associate with one another, become friends. Early into their semester-long terms of office, we see them hanging out together outside of student government, often countering strong norms whereby juniors and seniors rarely befriend sixth or seventh graders. Instead, we see male and female representatives forge platonic friendships. The lottery brings them together, and student government provides a cover from the teasing and gossip that often undermines such efforts.

I have had to silence the student government WhatsApp groups on my phone because they are constantly abuzz with many teenage jokes, memes, and music videos.

Although their work primarily focuses on serious, school-wide initiatives, they seem most excited when organizing smaller after-school activities just for student government members. So far, these have included potlucks, karaoke, soccer games, board games, a trip to the movies, and even a Saturday hiking trek into the nearby mountains.

Of course, not everyone gets along. There are many disagreements and even occasional spats. But on the whole, it has been striking to see how tight their bonds become and how long these bonds last, which often persist years after their term of office together has ended.

Diversity Is Key

Admittedly, it is difficult to definitively identify the key causes of these fast friendships.

It is true that many teenagers are innately curious and sociable. The experiences and achievements they share certainly strengthen their bonds—as does the leveling effect of lotteries (which I will explore in the next section).

However, having also worked with elected student governments and students in other contexts, it is clear to me that diversity is a key factor. When I watch them interact, they seem to be attracted to the novelty of conversations and connections they don't find in their cliques.

This all hit home for me recently while looking through some video footage from past years. I found a video with student representatives who were just finishing their term of office, in which I asked them what they liked most about the experience. Elvin, a sophomore, said it was "spending time together and making new friends." Stefani, a junior, backed him up, saying that what she liked the most was getting to know new people. Everyone agreed.

I asked them if they had known each other before this experience, and they all shook their heads. Then Adriana, a freshman, said, "I liked that we made great friends. We found ourselves thrown together with people that we didn't think we'd get along with." And when I asked them if they would enter subsequent lotteries, after a chorus of yeses, Adriana turned to her teammates and added, "But we all have to enter together!"

I often tout public speaking and facilitation, among the most important skills gained by students selected in student government lotteries. But in the end, for this next generation of citizens, the most important lessons might be the ones they enjoyed the most: learning how to get along with people who are different and seeing how enriching those interactions can be.

Lotteries as Levelers

Student Government Lotteries create and reinforce equality and cohesion among students.

When we help a school use lotteries instead of elections, for example, "losers" simply had bad luck and didn't have to feel publicly rejected by their peers. Likewise, it means that "winners" simply had good luck and have no reason to feel better than anyone else. The student government is formed without injuring or inflating anyone's ego and without fostering resentment or rivalries. In this way, student government lotteries serve as levelers.

Once the student government is formed, every member takes turns facilitating meetings, taking notes, and addressing the school. Each of them has the opportunity to learn and practice the related skills, and no one is excluded.

There are, however, a few responsibilities that require a designated person who can be held accountable, such as treasurer and coordinator. A conventional approach would be to have the group elect these positions, but what information would the new representatives use to pick among themselves?

Most don't know each other, having just been selected randomly from different classrooms and grade levels. Thus, they would almost undoubtedly choose the peer who seems most responsible to be treasurer and the one who is confident and charismatic to be a coordinator.

However, as I explained earlier, those biases are often misguided. Moreover, this approach can give chosen students an inflated sense of importance and those who were passed over feelings of rejection. So how do you think these responsibilities are distributed? You guessed it! Through lotteries.

A New Approach to Democracy

All those in the student government who want to be treasurer raise their hands.

If there is only one, the matter is done. If there are two, they flip a coin or play rock, paper, scissors. If there are more, they put names in a hat.

It is important to understand that if the selected student does not take their role seriously, the group can vote them out at any time. But the point is that no one who wants to learn a skill set or take on a responsibility is written off and denied an opportunity.

Within student government, the leveling effects of lotteries prevent feelings of superiority, inferiority, and resentment. This leads to a dynamic of equality that permeates student governments and is clearly valued by the students themselves.

Creative Uses of Student Lotteries

Students have even gone beyond our proposed uses of lotteries and employed them in other creative ways to maintain equality and cohesion.

One student government, for example, was working to reforest part of their school grounds and had secured a sizable donation of saplings. But only a couple of representatives could ride along to the nursery to select the different varieties of plants. Everyone wanted to go. So, without hesitation, one of them flipped over their hat while another marked different pieces of paper. Finally, the papers were folded up, thrown in the hat, and they all tried their luck.

Conversely, a student government at another school needed two of its members to take on a necessary task that nobody wanted. So instead of applying peer pressure or arguing, they drew green and purple beans from an urn. Even the unfortunate 'winners' had fun with it.

These diverse applications of lotteries reinforce the equality with which students interact and the cohesion of these diverse student governments. Of course, it's never perfect, but it goes a long way as these diverse groups of young people learn how to work together.

Adam Cronkright is a pioneering advocate for a better approach to democracy. He co-founded and led Democracy-in-Practice, whose work reinventing student government with democratic lotteries was a finalist for the Council of Europe's 2016 Democracy Innovation Award. He now co-leads of by for*. Debuting in 2023, the organization's documentary shows what happens when everyday citizens are called upon to serve, through a democracy lottery to make our most important decisions.

4

Governance

Western democracies are sputtering. What should be matters of public health or science twist into political issues that further divide and alienate communities.

One solution gaining traction among political theorists and concerned citizens is gradually decreasing the number of elected positions while increasing opportunities for participatory decision-making. We call it "Governance."

Of the six societal facets, governance is the "one ring to rule them all," to use a *Lord of The Rings* analogy. Without including participatory decision-making in fulfilling society's needs, communities become isolated, divided, and antagonistic—much of what we're seeing in the world now.

Participatory decision-making, as part of governance, has a menu of options. This section examines deliberative democracy, sortition, and citizens' assemblies.

Deliberative democracy is a school of thought that claims that political decisions should be the product of fair and reasonable discussion and debate among citizens, according to *Britannica*.

"In deliberation, citizens exchange arguments and consider different claims that are designed to secure the public good," Britannica states. "Through this conversation, citizens can come to an agreement about what procedure, action, or policy will best produce the public good."

Sortition chooses public officials by lot and is based on a political method used in ancient Greek city-states.

A citizens' assembly is a body formed from randomly selected citizens to deliberate on an important issue. Its purpose is to recruit a cross-section of the public to study the options available to the state on certain questions and propose answers to these questions through rational and reasoned discussion.

The following essays explore the ingredients necessary for governance in a restorative community and its implementation adjacent to the current political structure. We also feature experts in the field who are transforming their communities through governance.

How to Spend $20 Billion:
A True Representative Approach
to Crafting State Budgets

The coffee tasted like a burnt rope.

It was one of the few legal options available to keep me awake during the slog of the state budget meeting. We sat in the fluorescent-lit, cavernous committee room for hours, while government bureaucrats in drab suits explained how those in power wanted to spend the public's money.

I was a reporter then and had already skimmed the 500-page budget document, looking for local angles to write about for the next day's paper. There wasn't much. Despite vociferous claims by its authors to the contrary, the state budget proposal contained nothing new—just the usual stew of modest pay raises for teachers and state employees, a slight reduction in the corporate tax rate, cuts for outdated programs, and new line items to pay for the governor's pet projects.

True Representation: The Missing Ingredient

The missing ingredient was the voice of the people.

The state budget is an essential piece of legislation lawmakers pass, but most people don't know what's in it unless a controversial line-item grabs headlines. As a result, we pay taxes with the vague notion that our money will pay for things that keep our community running, like salaries for teachers and police, fixing the highways, or making sure public buildings are safe. But we have no real say in how our tax dollars are spent.

Government transparency often happens after the fact. A state budget proposal, for example, is posted *after* legislative leaders have sliced and allocated funding and programs. Citizen input through town hall meetings and "Tweet-ups" occurs *after* substantive decisions are made. Even efforts to solicit public feedback through online budget simulation exercises exclude the "real" factors in crafting a budget. These factors include the political ideology of those in power, upcoming elections, the wishes of campaign contributors, and changing voter demographics.

What Is True Representation?

I was skeptical when Ted first mentioned the idea of "True Representation." It is a concept that seeks to redefine how governance is done by creating local, state, regional, and national "citizens' assemblies," whose members are randomly selected. However, the more I explore the idea, the more I see its wisdom.

In his book, *True Representation*, Ted describes what conditions are necessary for good group decision-making. These are conditions such as access to timely, accurate information, diversity of opinion, independence of judgment, and decentralized decision-making. He also outlines the "House of Citizens" proposal for the United Kingdom as a "real-life" example. A statistically representative group of citizens could influence legislation approved by the elected House of Commons.

What If We Have True Representation?

What would be the outcome if large groups of ordinary, thoughtful citizens decided how taxpayer dollars are spent, instead of politicians?

Would teachers be paid a fair and living wage? How would we pay for healthcare for the poor, elderly, chronically ill, and children? Would we invest in preventative care, or would we continue the current path of crisis care that happens daily in emergency departments across the country?

Would we maintain regulations to ensure clean air and water, or would we see them as barriers to business development? Would we use public money to recruit businesses to the state through tax incentives, create incentives for existing businesses, or allow free enterprise to run without government interference? What would we as a society value, and how would we demonstrate it by the way we allocate public money?

Democracy Is Not a Spectator Sport

These are the critical questions of our time, even if they aren't discussed and debated on social media and cable news programs. We can no longer punt the answers to these questions to people, however well-meaning, who have twin goals of public service and maintaining power through re-election. We cannot treat democracy as a spectator sport, endorsing ridiculous policies offered by the political party we like and rejecting sensible ones we despise.

The future of democracy—whether we live in Baltimore or Brussels—depends on citizens' assemblies coming together, putting their differences aside, and working toward common-sense solutions that benefit everyone. Without True Representation, we'll continue to live in societies where fear is allowed to place barbed-wire fences on our borders and in our hearts.

If a group of ordinary, informed, thoughtful citizens gather to decide, for example, how to spend $20 billion in state funds and resources, maybe we'll have better coffee in the committee rooms.

What Happens When You Take Politics Out of Policy?

A Texas resort with cowboy-themed rugs, ten restaurants, and an indoor river walk housed an American democratic experiment in September 2019.

It was the latest in a series of more than a hundred such experiments in 28 countries Dr. James Fishkin, a Stanford University professor, and his colleagues have conducted over nearly 30 years. But this one was covered by *New York Times* reporters Emily Badger and Kevin Quealy.

"The voters arrived from all over the country: nine of them named John, ten who'd come from mobile homes, four who lived in South Dakota," Badger and Quealy wrote. "Twenty-seven considered themselves conservative; 30 said they were extremely liberal. Twenty-one were out of work and looking for it. Two came with service dogs."

America in One Room

Called "America in One Room," the deliberative polling experiment invited a cross-section of 526 people representing the voting public.

Participants were initially polled via phone about their political views, and invited to spend an all-expenses-paid weekend in a resort outside Dallas, to discuss their views on the Affordable Care Act and immigration.

Organizers gave participants a non-partisan, 55-page briefing book, which outlined the issues without the dog whistles and increasingly divisive political rhetoric. Then, participants were divided into smaller groups to discuss the issues. Finally, organizers again polled attendees after the weekend to see if their views had changed.

Fishkin and colleague Larry Diamond contend their experiment proves that when you put a diverse group of people together in a setting without political soundbites and tribal cues, voters are "likely to mute their harshest views and wrestle more deeply with rebuttals. As a result, they become more informed, even more empathetic."

Why We Need Deliberative Polling Now

As this book was being written, such experiments were gaining traction during the [first] presidential impeachment hearings of Donald Trump, and the 2020 election loomed over the horizon.

People say they want a return to civil discourse, but they don't know how. Experiments like Fishkin and Diamond's are about more than learning to agree to disagree. Deliberative polling, community processing, and citizens' assemblies are part of the restorative practices continuum. The continuum also includes informal processes such as restorative statements and questions, and circles; and other, more formal conflict resolution processes, as we saw in the "learning" section. Together, the processes that form the restorative practices continuum fill a gap in how large groups can overcome disagreements, and make meaningful and satisfying collective decisions.

Therefore, deliberative polling is essential in building a new reality. It has the potential to revitalize culture, improve public discourse, and generate better solutions to our most urgent problems because it relies on the collective wisdom of an informed crowd.

American society will not be sustainable in the long run, for example, if people refute scientific findings because those findings don't conform to their ideological views. Nor will we have a future if our response to the presence of Black and brown people is to call the police or put immigrant children in cages.

A Funny Thing Happened on the Way to Deliberative Polling

Unlikely pairings across racial and age divide sprung up during the weekend without moderators and guided discussions.

A Black, 24-year-old cashier from Michigan became close to three 70-year-old white men in his group. A 69-year-old retired nurse bought a birthday drink for a woman who turned 35 that day. Instead of shouting—as we're accustomed to seeing on social media, television, and Thanksgiving tables across the country—participants brought their life experiences and observations to bear on policy issues. They used personal stories to undergird their arguments.

Some participants didn't change their opinions on issues, despite building a rapport with people of opposing opinions. Others did. As a group, the voters shifted more toward the center, "in ways that can't be explained by typical polling movement over time."

One could argue that changing hearts and minds wasn't the point of the "America in One Room" experiment. Currently, people use news and information to confirm their bias, not change it or learn from it. That may not change soon, but we still have to live together on the same planet. Maybe the point is America could be great if its people stopped listening to talking points that reflected their fears, and started listening to each other.

America's Addiction to Voting

Americans are addicted to the idea of voting.

Voting represents ownership of the public policy and lawmaking processes. It denotes exclusive (citizen) membership in the American experiment of democracy. African Americans and women have died for the right to vote.

Recently, however, voting has become performative. We like to be seen doing it. So, we snap selfies wearing "I Voted" stickers and post on social media to brag and encourage others to vote. But once the sticker peels and our post fades into Facebook memory, we hand over important decisions about healthcare, education, public safety, and the environment to a handful of winners of a high-stakes popularity contest.

What if public policy and decision-making could be genuinely democratic and inclusive? What if you didn't delegate public policymaking to a chosen few? What if you had a direct say in what kind of community you want to live in?

Intriguing Possibilities

Brett Hennig, Anke Siegers, and Gert Jan Slump presented intriguing possibilities for participatory decision-making at the IIRP Europe Conference held in May 2019 in Kortrijk.

IIRP is the world's first accredited graduate school dedicated to researching and teaching restorative practices. Its conferences take a multi-disciplinary approach to discovering the common threads for improving civil society. The role of restorative practices in developing resilience and supporting well-being in communities and organizations was the focus of this year's conference.

Brett, Anke, and Gert are making significant advances to foster participatory decision-making, one of the chief aims of Building a New Reality. We highlight their work here to start a conversation about redefining how governance is done. We believe that large groups of ordinary citizens can make thoughtful, informed decisions about complex problems under the right conditions. The following sections feature two examples.

All Politics Are Local

Community Processing is the brainchild of Anke and Gert, experts in organizational change, conflict resolution, and restorative justice.

"In Holland, we have a lot of governments that say, 'we make the decisions, and you deal with the consequences,'" Anke said.

Community processing helps large groups with divergent and opposing interests come together and work collectively toward positive solutions. It creates a safe space for people to tell their stories and be heard. It also cultivates shared ownership and responsibility for the outcome, because everyone has an opportunity to be involved in the decision-making process. Community processing groups can be as small as 50 and as encompassing as a couple of thousand.

"We are not afraid the group will be too large," Anke said. "We leave many people out of (most) decision-making processes. If you ignore the minority voice, it is said you plant the seed for resistance."

Here's how community processing works—Anke and Gert help the group define the issue with a central, overarching question. Next, the group decides the legal and financial boundaries of proposals. Next, independent facilitators ask questions for further information gathering, such as "Who else needs to be involved?" and "What information needs to be presented at the gathering?" Finally, they use this information to gather in circles to discuss the issues, make concrete agreements, and establish follow-up appointments.

Anke and Gert recently used the process to help a community in Holland faced with a local hospital closing. First, it took facilitators six weeks to prepare for the participation of 2,300 people throughout the community in the decision-making process. Then, after intense group discussions, the groups spent 15 hours devising a solution that addressed the underlying issues of healthcare and shared values. The hospital was able to reopen.

Do Democracy Differently

Brett is a former astrophysicist turned social revolutionary, though he might bristle at me calling him that.

As the co-founder and director of the Sortition Foundation, Brett spearheads campaigns throughout Europe and the United Kingdom to "institute the use of stratified, random selection (also called 'sortition') in government." He proposes to "do democracy differently," by using random selection to populate assemblies or fill political positions.

"Everyone thinks voting equals accountability, but that's not true," Brett said. "Accountability is much more complex."

Sortition is the selection of political officials through a random sample from a larger pool of candidates. It is designed to empower citizens and remove the toxicity of politics from public policy-making.

"An assembly that uses sortition would be composed of people like you and me," Brett said. "It would be a representative random sample of people, making decisions in an informed, fair, and deliberative setting."

An assembly of 100 Irish citizens, for example, met in recent years to address the challenges and opportunities of the local aging population, climate change, abortion, gay marriage, and fixed-term parliaments. Conclusions and recommendations reached on each topic were compiled in a report and submitted to lawmakers to create legislation reflecting the report and then to voters in a public referendum.

The challenges of sortition as a deliberative decision-making process include convincing lawmakers to concede their power, recruiting interested participants, ensuring diversity and inclusion, and keeping lawmakers accountable to citizens' assemblies.

"The people who go through this (sortition process) are very honored," Brett said. "They come out transformed in the short-term. They come out more politicized. They say, 'my voice matters; now what?'"

The Magic of Sortition

When Ted first mentioned "sortition," I thought he was referring to the magical hat in the Harry Potter novels and movies, used to sort Hogwarts students into their appropriate houses. Turns out sortition is "the use of random selection to populate assemblies or fill political positions." Or as Sortition Foundation co-founder and director Brett Hennig explained, "An assembly that uses sortition would be composed of people just like you and me. It would be a representative random sample of people, making decisions in an informed, fair, and deliberative setting."

One of the aims of sortition is to create a better governmental decision-making model by removing the tedious, expensive, and increasingly offensive campaign process, endless need for fundraising, and the crushing influence of special interest groups. Sortition sounds great in a broad-minded discussion of democratic theories over a couple of pints in a pub sort of way. But how would it work in the real world?

A Sortition Skeptic

For nearly two decades, I have witnessed and participated in many facets of U.S. public policy, governance, and electioneering.

I have watched local school boards enact policies and procedures, reported on presidential campaigns from the front lines, developed and implemented communications strategies for political parties and candidates, lobbied on behalf of school choice organizations, and created innovative programs to increase fundraising among diverse political constituencies.

Therefore, the concept of sortition—using random selection rather than relying on strategy, messaging, money, and influence to sway political outcomes—seemed antithetical to my entire professional career up until two years ago. Of course, I resisted and sent Ted a detailed memo of all the reasons I thought sortition wouldn't work. Ted convinced me to read the research and reconsider my position.

Politicians, despite the narratives played out in traditional and social media, can gather to make intelligent, insightful, fact-based decisions that take the needs, desires, and aspirations of the public into account. I observed this firsthand, while reporting on the North Carolina Senate's floor debate on legislation that proposed ending the state's death penalty for two years, while they studied the economic, racial, and geographic disparities in capital sentencing. The arguments for and against the measure weren't based on ideology or scoring political points in the media, but on the information at hand and the potential impact on the integrity of the justice system. While the state senate approved the bill, it was later defeated in the state House.

If a group of seasoned politicians—ones with loyalties to constituencies, political parties, and donors—can make reasoned, intelligent decisions, could we have a fairer society if a group of people without such constraints made public policy decisions?

A Sortition Solution

Implementing sortition on a national level such as the U.S. Senate, as Brett and others have suggested, is too drastic and overwhelming. Such a change will be met with natural and sometimes irrational resistance to the way things "have always been."

I support those who want to experiment with sortition on a state level before using it to decide national matters. This "scaling up" of sortition helps acclimate the public to a different form of democracy, work out the inevitable kinks in the new system, and add some layer of accountability to the current public policymaking system.

I encourage creating sortition groups of citizens to advise state lawmakers on matters such as education, healthcare, the environment, infrastructure, and taxes. Some legislatures have such citizen-working groups, often called "Blue Ribbon Commissions." However, the difference between a Blue Ribbon panel and a sortition group is the sortition group would be randomly selected, rather than a *Who's Who* of political donors and allies, chosen by the legislative body to which it ultimately answers. Four sortition groups would meet quarterly to decide on a range of issues within their policy area. Depending on the complexity and urgency of the issue, the sortition group would have two to four weeks to consider the facts and make a series of recommendations to the legislature, based on the evidence.

Sortition members would be barred, much like jurors, from being influenced by outside groups. Their room, board, meals, and daily expenses would be paid for through public taxes, much the way state and federal lawmakers receive daily allotments, and their jobs would be secured during their time of service. State lawmakers would be required to implement the sortition group's recommendations into the proposed legislation, should it be approved; and to provide a detailed, accessible, easy-to-understand analysis, should it decide to go against the sortition group's recommendations.

Much like special interest groups that evaluate politicians based on how often they supported or opposed the organization's key initiatives, state lawmakers under a modified sortition system would be graded by how often they voted with and against the sortition group's recommendations. Voters could use the grading system to help them evaluate for which candidates they should cast their ballots.

The Magic of Sortition

Perhaps my suggested framework elicits more questions than it answers.

I am sure anyone can poke a million holes in my theory. But instead of talking about why things won't work, let's discuss possibilities to make it work. While sortition can't solve all the human errors of the democratic process, it can be a path to achieving the everyday magic that happens when a group of concerned, enlightened citizens come together to build a new reality.

Can Citizens' Assemblies Repair Our Broken Democracy?

The following is an interview with Brett Hennig, author of The End of Politicians: Time for a Real Democracy, *that I conducted some months after meeting him at the IIRP conference in Belgium.*—KB

Kerra: How does an astrophysicist become the head of the Sortition Foundation?

Brett: The first thing that got me on the streets was the Iraq War. I started linking things up and got involved with a refugee justice group. I joined a political party, saw the insides, and got disillusioned by the dominance of ego.

I saw that it was about keeping and maintaining political power, above all else. Anything considered an ethical consideration was rejected in the name of keeping political power. This was in Australia, although I lived in the U.K. and Europe.

In addition, I read *Multitude: War and Democracy in the Age of Empire,* by Michael Hardt and Antonio Negril, in 2016 and had an *"Aha!"* moment. I said, "Okay, democracy can be done differently." The history of democracy is always changing and evolving.

I was also looking for an organization or something to join, and looking for a book to read. I couldn't find one, so I wrote my own. As I kept reading more and more about it, I put it (the book) together. It took me over 10 years to get it published. It was published in 2017. In 2015, I set up the Sortition Foundation as the book went through the editorial process. If you like the book, you could join the foundation.

Kerra: **What is sortition?**
Brett: It's the random selection of people to political positions or citizens' assemblies. "Citizens' assemblies" is becoming a mainstream term used more and more, especially in Europe.

Kerra: **Has the idea caught on?**
Brett: Many people dismiss it (sortition) as a crazy idea. People who are attracted by it are often disillusioned with modern politics. They see modern electoral politics as corrupted and disrupted by money and egos. Many of these people are already politicized and concluded that things need to change dramatically.

Kerra: **What is the hardest part about convincing people that sortition/citizens' assemblies work?**
Brett: Convincing people who are relatively political that it works and functions. The first comment is, "People are stupid." They (respondents) have axes to grind. You have to get beyond the first knee-jerk reactions.

Kerra: **What do you say to people like me—a Black woman from the United States—whose ancestors fought and risked their lives to vote, who have concerns that we will be left behind if sortition is instituted?**
Brett: The fight for the vote was absolutely crucial in establishing the principle of political equality among all people, especially in the U.S. for men and women of color. This was preceded by the fight for the vote for women in various countries, which was preceded by the fight to extend the vote beyond only wealthy men, both in the U.S. and elsewhere.

All these struggles were immensely important. However, although we have won the right to vote and theoretical political equality, we have lost the battle for political equality in practice.

Wealthy, white men overwhelmingly still hold power in the U.S. Sortition achieves a demographic representation. The number of people of color in such a legislature or congress would match the census statistics. Moreover, it could result in more people of color in such a legislative chamber than there are currently.

Kerra: **Is western democracy at a crossroads today?**

Brett: Something has happened in Europe, specifically in the U.K. Democracy has been in crisis for years. Nearly everyone you ask says democracy is broken—Trump, Brexit, the rise of populism in Europe. People say something is wrong.

Kerra: **Where are the "hotbeds" of citizens' assemblies now?**

Brett: A very well-publicized citizens' assembly in Ireland led to the referendum that removed the country's constitutional ban on abortion. In France, (President Emmanuel) Macron holds a citizens' assembly on climate change. Scotland is in the process of organizing two citizens' assemblies, and Ireland is holding its third on gender equality. The Irish example has led to around 10 city councils in the U.K. holding citizens' assemblies on climate change. So, these things are overlapping, and everyone is taking notice.

Kerra: **What do you say to people in the United States who don't think citizens' assemblies can happen there?**

Brett: They can and do happen in the United States, but on a smaller scale. There are many examples of citizens' assemblies happening in the United States. For example, there is Healthy Democracy in Portland, Oregon. They call them "citizens' juries" or "policy juries." They also include fewer people, around 20 or sometimes less. They are doing one (citizens' assembly) on the city council's wages in Milwaukie, Oregon.

The Jefferson Center in Michigan also runs citizens' or policy juries. Finally, James Fishkin's work, "America in One Room," was large, though I don't believe it was connected to political power.

The whole idea that the U.S. is the birthplace of democracy is also completely false. You can look at quotes from Madison and others arguing against "pure democracy" and arguing for a republican government.

There were, for example, property qualifications on the right to vote that resulted in only rich, white men being allowed to vote. In the first election in the U.S., only about six percent of the population could vote, so they called it a republic and not a democracy. Nevertheless, most Americans think the system is broken. They have low trust in government and think money and vested interests have corrupted—or at least grossly distorted— the system.

Kerra: **Does a citizens' assembly remove responsibility from elected officials?**
Brett: Some people would see it as an abdication of responsibility. One of the most common comments we receive is, "We already have a citizens' assembly. It's called Parliament or Congress."

But many politicians like citizens' assemblies because it gets them out of the fire. When voting on a complex, emotional issue such as abortion in Ireland, politicians can say, "We are following the informed will of the people." The same could be said of Macron's citizens' assembly in response to the yellow-vest movement, climate change protests. [The yellow vest movement was a series of populist, grassroots weekly protests in France that first began in November 2018, for economic justice and later included institutional political reforms.]

Citizens' assemblies are not opinion polls. You have to deliberate and discuss the issue in an informed and fair environment. But unfortunately, politicians are using it as a tool to gain legitimacy for some decisions they finally take.

Kerra: **Are there upcoming citizens' assemblies we should watch?**
Brett: There are many citizens' assemblies happening in the U.K. and Europe. There is a national citizens' assembly starting this Friday [January 24, 2020] on climate change, and how to get the U.K. to net zero emissions by 2050.

This citizens' assembly is meeting in Birmingham, England, for four weekends. There is another citizens' assembly on the rise of hate crimes in a borough of London. Other citizens' assemblies were about redeveloping town centers and having a healthy relationship with alcohol.

There is also another Irish Citizens' Assembly on gender equality. The French citizens' assembly is still going on—we'll see what happens and how Macron responds, but he has promised much. Will he listen and respond, or will he use it as a cover or talking point?

Kerra: How do you see citizens' assemblies interacting with existing political electoral structures?

Brett: We want to see citizens' assemblies become a permanent, institutionalized part of democracy. We want to see them move from "one-off" events to permanent chambers or standing committees. The Sortition Foundation is possibly about to launch a campaign to replace the House of Lords with a citizens' assembly.

In the German-speaking region of east Belgium, their elected chamber set up a second randomly selected "citizens' council" to sit alongside the elected chamber.

Kerra: What do you see as the future for citizens' assemblies?

Brett: I doubt that people would move to a pure sortition model in the near future, without elections at all. I foresee, at first, a bicameral system where one chamber is elected, and another is randomly selected. Then, you could compare the behavior and decisions coming from the two chambers. I think I know which chamber people would trust more. Then I believe we would move to a randomly selected model. I think that is a sensible strategy to push this idea forward.

Citizens' Assemblies are gaining traction in the United States, as Brett Hennig pointed out in the previous section. Johanna Lundahl, a writer and environmental justice advocate, explained the forces that brought together 100 randomly selected residents of Washington State to take action on climate change.—KB

Washington State Citizens' Assembly on Climate—Solutions By the People, For the People

By Johanna Lundahl

Five Washington state legislators, all committee chairs, have called for a Citizens' Assembly on Climate in fall 2020.

In a May 31 Op-Ed, they wrote, "Too often in Olympia [Washington's state capital], the debate around our response to climate change devolves into environmentalists versus big businesses, urban versus rural, Democrats versus Republicans. It would help us all bring more voices to the table to understand deeply held concerns, concerns about the status quo, and concerns about the policies proposed to fight climate change."

The Citizens' Assembly on Climate is a non-partisan, direct democracy process that will bring together roughly 100 randomly selected residents of Washington who demographically mirror the state in age, gender, ethnicity, education, and previous views on climate. Assembly members will come together online throughout several weekends to develop connections, learn from science and policy experts, deliberate on paths forward, and recommend policies to lawmakers.

In this case, the recommendations will be delivered to the Chairs of five House Committees, once agreed upon by the assembly participants. The legislators who authored the Op-Ed have promised to take climate law and policy recommendations seriously, and the Assembly's work will flow directly into the drafting of policies for the 2021 Washington Legislative session.

A key event development in September 2019, the Protectors of the Salish Sea—a group of Indigenous organizers also known as "Water Protectors"—held a sit-in, in front of the Capitol Building in Olympia. They called on Governor Jay Inslee, the self-proclaimed Climate Governor, to end any new fossil fuel project permitting and convene "a special session on climate change that includes the voices of the youth, Indigenous Peoples, and those most affected by the climate crisis." Their six-month vigil ended in March 2020, when they left the capitol in response to the ongoing coronavirus pandemic.

Climate activist Michael Foster decided to attend Climate Assembly Washington, an informal group passionate about the opportunity to expand democratic methods to address the climate crisis. With the example of France's and the U.K.'s national climate change assemblies in mind, the group began working to introduce the concept of a Citizens' Assembly on climate to Washington lawmakers, stakeholders, and potential funders.

Citizens' Assemblies are not well known in the United States. However, the use of deliberative democracy in public forums was actually invented here in the 1970s. The Jefferson Center began to design and regularly operate citizens' juries in 1971. In addition, Stanford professor James Fishkin's deliberative polling techniques have been used since the 1990s to understand what conclusions the public might reach about a topic if they had the opportunity to become fully informed and engaged.

If carried out correctly, a Citizens' Assembly process can break through the standoff of opposing interests. Mirroring the origins of the democratic process from ancient Greece, the Assembly participants are chosen by lot and serve only once. The makeup of an assembly should perfectly reflect the population of the larger public, effectively creating a mini-version of the state, country, or city from which it is convened. The random selection process ensures a representative population.

Climate Assembly Washington hopes that the Assembly will generate actionable and exciting solutions for lawmakers by directly engaging Washington residents. The group itself will step aside at the point where a neutral organization, experienced in managing a project as timely and delicate as a climate assembly, will coordinate the project. The group advocates for a process, not an outcome, as it is appropriate for the state's citizens to determine the best steps forward.

The Washington activists asked the committee chairs of the committees in the state legislature to call for the Assembly, and they did so in their May 31st Op-Ed. Representative Ryu of the 32nd district is among those eager for the Assembly's recommendations to inform their work. As she wrote, "We must hear the authentic voices of Washington's residents, from indigenous communities to farmers and tech workers, to know what actions the people of our state recommend when they work together to create solutions."

Due to the COVID-19 crisis, the Assembly will now be completely online. Efforts will be made to ensure equal access to participation, with the additional needs of providing access to high-quality internet and equipment to ensure that even those with few resources can participate. The Assembly must also be broken up into shorter sessions and spaced out longer over time. Not many people can remain engaged over long hours online.

Big decisions lie ahead: about the design of the Assembly, who will coordinate it, and where all the funding will come from, but Climate Assembly Washington's goal is in sight.

With ongoing outreach to environmental organizations around the state, the group's following tasks include:

> Fundraising
> Facilitating the choice of coordinators
> Hosting a workshop to determine the specific focus of the Assembly

Donations to fund the event are coming from crowdfunding and major donors who are passionate about expanding democracy and agree to donate with no strings attached.

Washington State will be the first state to host an online Citizens' Assembly on climate this coming fall, providing another positive example of the Citizens' Assembly model for the country to learn from. Just as assemblies have spread across the U.K. and around Europe, deliberative democracy techniques can be used more widely across the United States to address the climate crisis. The greatest challenge of modern times requires the greatest resources available: the people—each able to share their perspectives and add to the expanded conversation.

Environmentalist author Bill McKibben has shared his excitement for the model. "As a rural New Englander, used to governance by Town Meeting, I'm excited by the prospect of these Citizens Assemblies: I know how much creativity and unity they will produce!"

Advocates say that it's time to have faith in the residents of Washington State. They understand the urgency of the situation and, given the opportunity to learn about and discuss potential solutions, expect them to respond with enthusiasm.

Johanna Lundahl is a writer and session aide to Washington State Representative Jake Fey, D-27. She previously served as a Communications Associate with a small nonprofit focused on political engagement, democracy, and environmental justice.

I wrote the following essay in 2020 at the start of the COVID pandemic in the United States. Isolation during the quarantine gave many people an opportunity to think about how we can best live together. For me, it starts with a "revolution by conversation."

I began this section with the "big" ideas of the restorative practices continuum. We discussed deliberative polling, sortition, and citizens' assemblies. However, there is also power in the small, daily actions we can take to make a difference.—KB

Starting a Revolution by Conversation

The COVID-19 virus forced a global slowdown in communities, schools, businesses, and financial markets as countries scrambled to contain the spread of the pandemic. With deep reverence and respect for those who are most at-risk of the disease and those at the frontlines of the virus, I hope the societal changes the pandemic engenders will spark a "revolution by conversation."

Social distancing and sheltering in place have become the new norm. Virtual potlucks, video conferencing, and online campfires replace how we live, work, and play.

And let's face it, there's only so much binge-watching you can do on Netflix, Amazon, and other streaming services. So, we will have to turn to each other and say something other than, "Can you pass the remote?"

Uncivil Discourse

Perhaps the crisis, as awful as it is, came just in time.

The social and public conversations about the issues that matter in the United States and elsewhere lacked two essential ingredients—civility and discourse. For example, during the Democratic presidential primary, supporters of various candidates blamed, bullied, and barked at each other to vote for their nominee and were frustrated when the tactic failed. But then, the same people lamented when the diverse field of candidates narrowed to two old, white men without asking why.

The "why" is crucial because it will tell us things we can never get from a poll, campaign ad, or talking heads segment. The underlying reasons reveal what we are concerned about, the country we hope to live in, and how we want to achieve shared goals.

Revolution by Conversation

Ted first introduced me to "revolution by conversation."

It's the idea, as Ted says, that "given the right context, ordinary people are capable of remarkable outcomes." Tools like participatory learning and decision-making, restorative practices, citizen assemblies, and deliberative democracy "represent a dramatic improvement in how human beings interact." One of Ted's chief aims is to achieve "democracy in everyday life" by listening to one another.

Revolution by conversation clicked for me when I read a social media post by a frustrated progressive friend who asked why her friends supported President Donald Trump for the umpteenth time. One person responded, "Because he's the only person who loves America and cares about America."

We can debate the truth of the commenter's statement. However, it would be more important to ask, "What does it mean to 'love' and 'care' about America? How do such sentiments benefit you and your family? How do you think it drives policy decisions? Why is it important to you?"

From their answers, we get more than a hillbilly elegy. We get what matters most to people and why they vault patriotism over the mountains of criticism at Trump during his presidency. His supporters aren't dumb or lacking a moral compass. We either have different values or different expressions of the same values. But we'll continue to be mired in tribalism if we don't talk to each other. Empathy is sorely missed in political and social discussions when one group of people ignores or dismisses others' concerns. There are emotional, physical, and financial needs often underscoring a person's political position that we won't know unless we ask. We cannot get to those answers through shaming, blaming, and lecturing.

A Pandemic Future

Whether the societal slowdown ignited by the COVID-19 global pandemic lasts for six weeks or six months, we will all be changed by it in unforeseen ways.

In the United States and other countries, the governmental and institutional responses to the virus reveal the societal fissures that have always been there but concealed under veils of busyness, social media, tribalism, and uncivil discourse.

We will create a new reality due to the pandemic through our daily actions and how we treat each other. The spread of and response to the virus prove we cannot function by remaining in ideological silos and hoping things will "just take care of themselves." In Ted's words, we must have a "revolution by conversation." Our very survival depends on it.

5

Care

The concept of "care" in society usually means doing things "for" people, not "with" them. Examples of this include institutions that care for "at-risk" or vulnerable populations.

However, in restorative communities we achieve better outcomes when affected individuals and their families can exercise their voice and have choice within the process of care. Simple mechanisms for using their voice include an interview to evaluate the care experience of nursing home patients and their families, or changing the environment in which individuals and families in crisis have conversations.

One of the things that struck me most about restorative practices in Kortrijk, Belgium, was the use of the natural environment as a source and co-conspirator in the healing process. Troubled youths and their families, for example, can discuss their issues on a nature hike as easily as in a nonprofit conference room or classroom.

The following section is composed of blog posts I wrote in 2019, after exploring community initiatives in Kortrijk and Detroit that exemplified restorative care. Those most affected were not defined solely by their problems, but participated in devising sustainable, effective solutions. I hope these stories encourage you to think of care more expansively. Healing can occur anywhere when we use our empathy and imagination.

Forta Kuné: Together We Are Stronger

A mother and son embark on a hiking trip.

The son loses his balance during a challenging vertical climb. His mother grabs him before he tumbles several feet below the rocky ground. Relieved that he is safe, she clutches him tight. It's been a long time since she held her son to her breast. She can still feel the little boy in the lean skeleton of the man he is becoming.

He shrugs off his mother. She's always holding on to him too tight. She constantly nags him about what he's doing, who he's with, and where he's going. Doesn't his mother understand he's a man now? He didn't want to come on this camping trip anyway. He misses his friends back in the city. He resumes the climb.

A Mother and Son Story

Hours later, the sun dips below the mountain peaks.

Mother and son join similar families around a campfire. Their muscles ache. But it's the good kind of tiredness, the soreness that comes from stretching and rebuilding lost muscle memory. Volunteer coaches trained in restorative practices guide the conversation around the day's events and insights gained. The light and heat of the campfire elicit radical honesty.

When it is her turn to speak, the mother says, "I know that you are a man now. But I am still your mother. I still need to hold you and know that you are okay."

"Your love suffocates me," the son responds with tears in his eyes. "I love you, but I need space to figure out who I am and what I want to do with my life."

She agrees to give him space. He agrees to allow her to hug and fuss over him occasionally. Finally, mother and son have clarity and understanding where there once was silence punctured by occasional fights.

Restorative Practices Meet Outward Bound

Wies Vandenbulcke told me the bare bones of the mother and son story on a cold, rainy morning in October.

He leads Forta Kuné, an experimental initiative in Kortrijk, Belgium, that combines family support counseling with wilderness experiences such as camping, hiking, and canoeing in the mountains. Deriving its name from an Esperanto phrase meaning "together strong," Forta Kuné is part of a constellation of programs administered by Oranjehuis. This local nonprofit organization adapts restorative practices to serve at-risk youth and families in West Flanders.

Forta Kuné focuses on families who want to actively work on creating sustainable parent and child relationships, by removing them from their old habits and environments.

"For example, if you have a father and son who fight, you may have a mother who is the peacemaker," Wies said. "If you exclude the mother, they have to go back to the basics with each other and in nature."

Every activity in the wilderness experience is designed for two people, such as kayaking or bicycling. A volunteer coach checks on the pair's progress and identifies practical challenges they encountered that can be used as springboards for further discussion. Together, they learn to develop a positive space where the parent and child can speak and be heard, respect each other's position, and create a path forward for the relationship.

"Sometimes it's easier to talk about something when you are doing something active together rather than sitting in a circle facing each other," Wies said. "It's restorative because they can restore their bond by doing things together. When a parent makes time for their child because they want to fix their broken relationship, it sends a powerful message."

Finding Meaning in Forta Kuné

We gloss over our parenting struggles in the United States by posting highlight reels of our families on social media.

In Belgium, I spoke to parents who meet once a month in frustration, humility, and grace to discuss their problematic relationships with their children. One mother showed the group a photo of her children calmly watching television. She said a year ago such a photo wouldn't have been possible due to the behavioral health issues of one of her children, which keep the rest of the family entangled.

Another parent showed me a photo of a meal that her teenage son had made earlier that week. They had been fighting for over a year. He couldn't say the words to reconnect, but he could cook a meal. A teenage girl told me that she felt unloved by her parents and was afraid to return to them after her stay at Oranjehuis ended.

These families are in crisis, but they are inching toward healing. I briefly share their stories here to show that they aren't different than you and me. We just don't talk about it, because we are afraid of being vulnerable, scared and less-than-perfect.

We often come to experimental models like restorative practices and participatory decision-making because we want tools to fix external circumstances—other people, broken families, corrupt systems.

However, the more I observe and engage with these models in Kortrijk, Detroit and in my own life, the more I realize that we can't change the world until we change ourselves. The macro and micro are interrelated. Thinking that there is no relationship between how we treat our children, and the people we elect who set policies that govern the care and education of all children and families, is where we run into trouble.

In visiting and writing about Forta Kuné, I realized its very name contains an essential message for building restorative communities: "Together, we are stronger."

Tilling the Soil of a New Reality: An Organic Farm in Belgium

"Welcome. What you pay attention to grows."
The battered, wooden sign greets visitors to De Heerlijkheid van Heule, an organic farm on the outskirts of Kortrijk, Belgium. Heerlijkheid van Heule roughly translates as "Glory of the Hill."

Operated by Oranjehuis, a group home for at-risk youth, the farm combines the simplicity and beauty of nature with a restorative framework to provide opportunities for youth and families in crisis and community engagement for the surrounding village.

"For me, the farm is where I can go, and I know that if I have a bad day, I will feel better," said Mattias, a tour guide at Heerlijkheid van Heule.

There were many dark days in Mattias's past. Mattias's easy smile and warm demeanor belie that he grapples with behavioral health issues and is on the autistic spectrum. Before his 18th birthday, he was shuffled in and out of several hospitals and contemplated suicide. Then, one day, Mattias visited an open house at Heerlijkheid van Heule held for the local community. He instantly felt at home.

"Just being at the farm helps me," said Mattias, now 24 years old. "The place itself is peaceful and quiet."

A Restorative Approach to Farming

Heerlijkheid van Heule is a working farm and restorative recreational center.

Oranjehuis bought the sustainable farm in mid-2005 with the help of the local, Flemish community. The farm's caretakers and neighborhood volunteers employ a restorative approach to organic farming by maintaining respect for people, animals, and the environment. The farm offers natural products from planting seeds to processing vegetables and doesn't use pesticides or other processing agents.

The farming of West Flemish red cows, grain cultivation and bread processing, and growing vegetables are among the farm's chief agricultural activities. The agricultural facets of Heerlijkheid van Heule cover approximately 8.5 hectares, half of which consists of arable land. The smaller half comprises low meadows that form a flood basin for the Heulebeek, a significant stream in West Flanders. The wettest part of the meadows at Heerlijkheid van Heule is developed as a nature preserve.

Visitors of all ages can walk around and through the farm—an interactive footpath, a walkway that crosses a lilting stream, and beautiful views of protected farmland. In addition, community events featuring entertainment and delicious Belgian dishes prepared with food grown on the farm are held throughout the year.

"We invite people to come and work in nature," said Stijn Deprez, director of external communications for Ligand, a restorative practices training organization that partners with Heerlijkheid van Heule and Oranjehuis. "In the city, it's very busy. Here, we help people get calm."

Families in Crisis

The promise of technology to create a global community has divided families—one in which screens have taken the place of conversations. Stagnated wages, a worsening housing crisis, and the growing influence of drugs and social media compound things for struggling families. In addition, an influx of refugee children who have fled dangerous situations that no child should see add another level of complexity.

"The behavior of the youngsters illustrates the problems in the community," said Michael Michiels, an administrator at Ligand, a restorative practices training center in Kortrijk. "They are the most vulnerable in our community and show us the problems in the community."

Ligand and its affiliates, such as Oranjehuis and Heerlijkheid van Heule, have stepped into the breach. The organizations apply a restorative practices framework to programs, services, and public spaces that help youth, families, and communities repair harm, restore broken relationships, and build social capital.

"If you don't work with the family, the problems will continue," Michael said. "We work with families, schools, and sometimes we work with the whole neighborhood. There are people from everywhere working together."

Cultivating a New Reality

The approach to restorative practices in Kortrijk happens actively and in nature.

Activity and nature loosen the grip of behavioral patterns and provide space for observation, insight, and new possibilities. This approach allows us to deepen our connections between ourselves and others in a setting that stimulates openness and understanding. This potent combination also allows for an individual as well as collective change.

We build a new reality not by forcing the world to conform to our whims; but by intentionally changing the DNA of our perceptions and behaviors. Places of restorative intention like Heerlijkheid van Heule allow that to happen.

"Even if you have a bad day, you can always learn something," said Mattias about a recent experience working at the farm. "Yesterday, I learned that not everything I think is what it seems."

Mattias struggles with overthinking and exaggerating as part of his autism diagnosis. He also struggles to be social. However, the tranquility of Heerlijkheid van Heule led Mattias to discover new parts of himself, like his facility with languages. Once silenced by the facilities responsible for his care, Mattias speaks four languages fluently and now gives tours at the farm.

"In the city, I feel small," Mattias said. "I don't look around. So, when I come here, I straighten my back."

How Circle Rituals Can Build Community Resilience

I felt Johan's absence in the empty spaces between Kristin Verellen's words.

Kristin was a keynote speaker during the opening session of the International Institute for Restorative Practices (IIRP) Europe Conference. The audience of leaders, practitioners, changemakers, scholars, and community advocates gathered at Buda Island in Kortrijk, Belgium, to learn more about using restorative practices to enhance community well-being and resilience.

A Belgian certified psychotherapist and coach, Kristin spoke in a lilting Dutch accent as she talked about the events of March 22, 2016.

Kristin remembered lingering in bed a while longer, savoring birthday wishes while her life partner, Johan Van Steen, went to work. Then, two explosions occurred at Brussels Airport in Zaventem an hour later. Shaken by the news, Kristin called Johan to discuss it. Then, the phone line went dead.

"It was three and a half days before I had any news of Johan," Kristin said. "The only news I had of him was that he's not on the list of the dead, and he's not on the list of the living."

While Johan was still reported missing, Kristin searched for him during the day and met with family and friends in the evenings.

"It started as a way of surviving, but then it became the most precious, human thing you can do at such moments," she said. "We sat down...in a circle just to come back to ourselves, to try to find the words for what we were feeling and try to make sense of it."

The nightly circle grew and even lasted after Johan was found dead in the rubble.

"At the start (of the circle group), there was a lot of heaviness," Kristin said. "But at the end, there was lightness, even laughter."

We Have the Choice

Kristin co-founded "We Have the Choice" in the aftermath of the terrorist attack.

The volunteer nonprofit "organizes moments of meaningful gathering in different circle formats, contributing to building a culture of inclusiveness and dialogue, healing trauma in people and communities, transforming powerlessness into strength, and connecting human beings from heart to heart."

Its name, "We Have the Choice," derives from Kristin's response to a reporter's questions about how the Brussels bombings affected her, given Johan's death.

She said: "The choice is pretty simple. Either we step onto the downwards spiral of violence that violence calls for, or we step onto the upwards spiral of violence that unlocks love. Love transcends everything."

Kristin and other facilitators at We Have the Choice guide circles at the request of organizations. Each person has a chance to speak and be heard in response to a question.

"It is not a dialogue—a circle," Kristin said. "We listen from the center. It's like listening with the ears of the group together. We speak from the heart. We leave the roles that everyone carries outside."

Special attention, Kristin said, is given to those groups in vulnerable situations that are an easy target when it comes to polarization and hardening, such as young people or the Muslim community.

"We are not a victim organization," Kristin said. "I want to support people to find their voice, to find their resilience again. It's also good to help people give voice to their feelings and stories."

The Prevalence of Trauma

This is the point in Kristin's story that we applaud.

We feel redeemed by a story in which the grieving loved one transforms her private pain into public healing because it gives us the illusion of triumphing over death. We remark on Kristin's generosity, courage, and resilience.

All are true. But Kristin's story is more than becoming an alchemist of our grief. It's also about addressing an epidemic in which the incidents upon which we are individually and collectively called to respond to trauma—our own or someone else's—are becoming increasingly common.

The Islamic extremists who perpetrated the Brussels bombings belonged to the same terrorist cell in the November 2015 terrorist attacks that devastated Paris a few months before. In the United States, there have been more than 140 mass shootings this year as of this writing.

Using circle rituals to address individual and community trauma runs contrary to societies that define inclusion by who we exclude, the walls we erect, and the porous borders we claim to protect in the name of freedom. Yet, we must swim against the tide of popular public opinion if we want a future.

Inviting the Unseen and Unspoken

Given the current environment of gun violence, political and social divisiveness, and movements toward nationalism and isolation, it's no longer a matter of whether you will experience trauma; it's when it will be your turn.

But loss and trauma can also occur at any stage of one's life and intensity.

Kristin underscored the point during her talk when she asked the audience to raise their hand if they had ever lost one or both of their parents or if they had ever lost the illusion of youth. A sea of hands appeared by the second question.

As practiced by Kristin and other facilitators in "We Have the Choice," Circle rituals are responsible and practical responses to loss and trauma that happen on the micro and macro levels because they create safe spaces for people to process trauma. They also help people feel less lonely and isolated.

"We invite what is unspoken, unseen, unprocessed— everything under the waterline," Kristin said. "It's only when we have access to that, that everything starts again to stream."

As Kristin concluded her talk—an artful combination of her narrative and Johan's photographs—the distance between the living and the dead, absence, and presence, narrowed. Then she read the following words from a poem she wrote to Johan shortly after his death:

My love
where can we go now with our lives?
I feel like drifting between this and the other side/
But no matter how deep the water
As long as we swim
We'll find
Each other.

Restoring Homes in Detroit

I was late for a meeting with Quincy Jones (not that one), and he was not happy about it.

"I thought you said you were coming at ten o'clock," he said, as we arrived an hour late.

Time was not a suggestion for Quincy. Lean, tall, and muscular, he had things to do. As the Osborn Neighborhood Alliance (ONA) executive director, Quincy helps children and families feel safe in their homes through community initiatives.

For Quincy, restorative communities begin at home.

"When I think about this work, I think of the physical environment because when you're worried about where you're going to live, it messes up everything," Quincy said. "That's what I think we have to stabilize and restore. People need a safe place to live."

The Home Depot of Human Services

The Matrix Community Center is the headquarters for Quincy's work.

Housed in a sprawling, repurposed church on East McNichols Road, the center offers services encompassing early childhood, homeless youth, youth and families in crisis, senior services, HIV/AIDS support, and a comprehensive Head Start program.

"We are the Home Depot of Human Services," Quincy said. "I love that the center is in the heart of the Osborn Community. It's walkable too. You can easily get to the library, the Dollar Store, and the funeral home."

Mortality was present that day in the Matrix Community Center and its unspoken goal of preserving life.

We threaded through a group of mourners as Quincy led us through a labyrinth of offices and meeting rooms. Dressed in stiletto boots and leather miniskirts that defied the mid-March chill, the bereaved women confronted death—a presence as familiar as the fast food and check-cashing places in strip malls dotted along the road.

"Restoring is about rebuilding, healing from whatever is happening, or reinventing yourself," Quincy continued. "How can I restore or improve myself if I'm broken?"

Restoring Brokenness

Quincy developed the "Live in Osborn" initiative as part of a decade-long effort to revitalize Detroit's struggling neighborhoods. Through a partnership with the city and other local nonprofits, the Osborn Neighborhood Initiative (ONA) adopted a cluster of land on Mapleridge Street, about two blocks from the Matrix Center.

ONA created a community park, boarded abandoned buildings, and renovated a three-bedroom, two-bathroom home on the corner. It was the first of eight homes to be renovated. ONA raised the money to restore the formerly abandoned home, which suffered from smoke damage, at about $55,000 and offered it for $60,000. The net $5,000 will be used to restore another home. By offering "rent to own" opportunities, Quincy wants to encourage Black homeownership to stimulate the local economy.

"During the mortgage crisis, many people lost their homes," Quincy said. "For black people, that was where we held most of our wealth. We want to restore that."

Someone Cares

Abandoned homes are a quiet obsession in Detroit.

City leaders, private investors, and economic developers tie the number of abandoned homes to Detroit's crime and unemployment rates.

Nearly one-third of the city's home stock is vacant. While Michigan's number of vacant homes dropped by four percent to 380,719 as the population slightly increased, the number of vacancies increased in Detroit by 29.5 percent. There were about 102,330 abandoned homes as of 2020 when the Center for Community Progress released a report on the topic. The organization is a leading national nonprofit that helps communities with property revitalization.

It isn't just the number of abandoned homes that concern Detroiters. It's what those numbers mean and what can happen inside the homes. Parents worry their children might get hurt playing inside abandoned buildings. Community residents and the police worry about drugs and criminal acts happening in the shell of abandoned homes. That's what makes boarding up and revitalizing abandoned homes even more critical.

"We want a spot where kids can feel safe," Quincy said. "We began doing board-ups. A board-up shows that there's some forward activity happening right now. It means we're going to close this building up so it can feel safe."

The community boarded up about one thousand windows in homes in one year. They also spent nearly $400,000 in the past five years, boarding up homes, including commissioning artwork on the blighted buildings. Critics say boarding up blight is a band-aid for a more significant problem. But for Quincy, a band-aid still counts.

"You can still say something is happening over here," he said. "There's someone or some organization that cares about this neighborhood."

6

Justice

The first impulse when a crime happens is to demand justice, which usually means punishment.

I am no exception. When white supremacists murder innocent Black people, I want them to get the death penalty. Wishing the deaths of those who harm Black people is corrosive to my spirit and well-being. Instead, "real justice" happens when we repair the harm caused by a crime.

Restorative practices provides an alternative or supplemental response to punishment. Restorative justice should routinely be available for the benefit of crime victims. Further, restorative justice offers victims, offenders, and their families and friends the opportunity to talk with one another, in a safe setting and with a competent facilitator to organize the process.

It can also be a community conversation, especially as residents devise policies to ensure public safety.

In a restorative community, justice employs restorative practices to reduce criminal reoffending and the impact of crime on victims and their communities of care.

But what happens when the criminal is a police officer? How do we find a path for healing when those sworn to "protect and serve" citizens violate them? Sadly, that's my story and that of hundreds, maybe even thousands, of Black and brown people living in communities plagued by militarized policing.

A valid criticism of restorative practices is that they don't address or advance the causes of social justice movements like Black Lives Matter. Critics argue that restorative practices don't provide a specialized framework to communicate across race, gender, or ethnic differences.

However, founders of this lineage of restorative practices never meant to apply them to social movements because at their inception they were focused on individual wrongdoing in schools and communities, not systemic oppression. Nevertheless, people adapt restorative practices to their needs.

The following section details my personal experience of race, its role in community policing, and strategies to shape a new social justice story in the United States.

Racism: America's Original Sin

Race shadows and illuminates my life. I know it's a social construct. Portuguese traders invented the concept of race in the 15th century to justify the capture, sale, and enslavement of Black bodies from west Africa to the Americas. These Black bodies were my ancestors. So, I can't just "let it go." Nor can I go along with the lie that America is a democracy. Slavery was carved into its bones.

Race in the United States is an economic proposition. Spurious medical science was invented to create a racial caste system in the United States that allowed white men to rape the Black women in their care. The children born from the rape could never inherit their white father's property. Instead, those children became part of their father's property—to be bought and sold at a whim.

Racism's Tentacles

The concept of race was designed to police the freedom of Black bodies and to separate them from white ones. We see the remnants of such a shameful legacy in nearly every sector of American life. It is reflected in the health of American citizens— who gets access to care and who is left to die. We also see racism's legacy in redlining, which determines where families can live and where children can go to school.

Race is harvested in the American education system. Public schools are funded, in part, by property taxes. "Separate but equal" laws were abolished nearly 70 years ago. But the American school system is far from equal. Even with the advent of bussing and integrated schools, Black children still face harsher disciplinary treatment than their white peers. It created a school-to-prison pipeline that runs just as cavernous and slippery as the Trans-Alaska Pipeline.

Most horrifically, we see the tentacles of America's racist legacy in the militarized policing of Black and brown communities.

The modern American policing system, which I'll discuss in more depth later, was fashioned when Northern cities recruited Southern police officers, often KKK members, because they knew how to "handle" Black populations.

Fatal police shootings are on the rise. The number of fatal police shootings increased from 1,021 in 2021 to 1,055 in 2022, despite increased public awareness of police brutality, stunningly demonstrated in the death of George Floyd in 2020. Moreover, the rate of fatal police shootings among Black Americans was much higher than that for any other ethnicity, standing at 38 fatal shootings per million of the population as of May 2022, according to Statistica, a research service that tracks public data.

Why the Political Is the Personal

I take the political personally. I knew what the word "nigger" meant before I mastered long division. Maybe I heard my dad or uncle say it on occasion with a mixture of awe and ridicule. Or maybe I heard the word mixed with a killer beat and laconic lyrics rapping about urban Black life like it was a pirate's tale.

But never did I imagine that I was a "nigger" until I was called one by a white boy while at the school playground. The word assassinated any high opinions I had of my intelligence and self-worth. None of that mattered now. What was I going to do?

I surveyed the options like a character in the "Choose Your Adventure" books that were popular in the 1980s. We lived in Camden, New Jersey, a small enclave across the Delaware River from Philadelphia. Campbell's Soup, a long-time employer in the city, had shifted most of its operations elsewhere after they stopped using the tomatoes South Jersey was famous for, in favor of California tomato paste. Crack cocaine dripped in from Philadelphia and New York. Violence spiked with rising unemployment and an easy flow of drugs. My choices were few—drug dealer, pregnant teen, or nerd.

My parents weren't much help. They didn't greet my tears about being called a "nigger" with cuddles and pie. They prophesied that my white schoolmate would be the first in a long line of white people who call me that word to my face or behind my back. Drug dealer and pregnant teen came with deadly side-effects. Instead, I doubled down on nerd.

College was the only way out. But there was no money to send me to school. So, I would have to earn a scholarship. While I ran track and played field hockey, I was far from an athlete. An academic scholarship was my only path. So, I treated school like a full-time job. I worked four times as hard to be considered twice as good as my white, male classmates.

But being smart and working hard didn't save me.

An Abuse of Power

On a sticky June afternoon one month before my 18th birthday, I was walking home from the library. I felt proud of myself because I finally pulled Toni Morrison's *Beloved* from the library stacks, after months of doubting whether I could handle its complex literary and spiritual texture.

My family measured time on summer afternoons by the weekday soap opera schedule. If *All My Children* is on, then it must be between 1 and 2 p.m. I promised Mom I would be home by *General Hospital*, which started at 3 p.m., to help make dinner. But on that day, I was late. I nearly ran into traffic when a police officer held his hand up.

The police officer surveyed the geography of my barely young adult body. He smiled and said, "I'd stop traffic for you anytime."

I returned his flinty smile with an awkward one and hurried inside.

The officer returned to my house for the next several days, often when my parents weren't home. A bicycle was reported stolen. A suspicious person was seen lurking around our backyard.

When the excuses failed him, he got to the point. He said he couldn't stop thinking about me. I needed to meet him at a corner the next day. He would take me to a place where we would "talk." If I refused, he would arrest my stepfather for drunk driving. He could also arrest my parents for smoking weed. The officer said he smelled it when he came to our house. Those were the days when a few ounces of weed could land you a five-year sentence or more.

Retreating in Silence

My parents didn't deserve to pay for my "sins"—though I can't tell you what transgression I committed.

Reading Toni Morrison? Wearing bike shorts and an oversized t-shirt on a grimy, summer day? Being a young Black girl in a world where white men can and did take whatever they wanted.

Even if I couldn't recall the exact nature of the sin, it was mine alone to bear. I "let" the officer take me. I didn't respond to his efforts at small talk as if what happened was consensual. I nodded when my parents asked if I enjoyed the library that day.

I wrapped my silence around me like prayer beads as the social worker asked my confused and heartbroken parents why I tried to run away from home a few weeks later. I met their tears and pleas with silence.

A month later, I packed my belongings and headed to college to start a new life. I avoided going home by getting jobs during holiday breaks and throughout the summer. I finally returned to my parents' home two years later when they moved to another town.

Some would say race had nothing to do with what happened with the police officer. But they're wrong. He chose me because history told him that I would not, could not, fight back. He knew that as a white man, his word would be taken over mine. I want a world where the men sworn to protect and serve citizens wouldn't rape them. I want a world where I could forgive my 17-year-old self for making the best decision she could under such horrific circumstances.

Can Restorative Practices Save Black Lives?

The last place I wanted to be was at a Community-Police Summit. My encounter with the traffic cop happened decades ago. But I live in the shadow of it. I don't allow men to get close to me. As a result, I freeze up when seeing a police officer. Instead, the body remembers what the heart wants to forget.

Unresolved anger and trepidation wrestled in my stomach on the morning of the summit, along with the last swallows of McDonald's coffee.

Despite the June heat, a chill wrapped my bones as I watched police officers from Detroit's Fifth District file in the room. Some officers mingled with the public at the back tables stacked with doughnuts, more coffee, orange juice, and pastries.

Ted commissioned me to visit Detroit and write a series of articles about Black-led, grassroots efforts in Detroit to implement restorative practices in nearly every city sector, including community policing. I wonder if Ted knew how Detroit would change me or if it was just a lucky guess.

Detroit is fertile ground for restorative practices because of its rich yet troubled history, population, diverse cultures, location, and significance in regional and national economies. Moreover, nearly 80 percent of the city's residents are Black. Restorative practices can repair harm, restore relationships, and build social capital in communities historically plagued by racism, unemployment, poverty, and violence.

Residents can use tools like Community-Police Summits to transform law enforcement from an institution that imposes itself on their daily lives to one that helps them co-create safe neighborhoods. That was the idea of the summit, explained Commander Eric Ewing.

"We want police officers getting into neighborhoods and knowing the people they're serving," Commander Ewing said. "So, we came up with a program to reach out to the public and say, 'hey, we recognize we don't do a good job of explaining why we do what we do.' We want to get the citizens in here to find out if there's something we could have done better."

Transforming Community Policing

Inspired by a procedural justice class offered five years ago by the Chicago Police Department, Commander Ewing developed a program that trains police officers in restorative practices.

The program also sponsors meetings or "summits" throughout the city. Police officials invite citizens who have filed complaints against a specific police officer to attend and share their grievances. The officers also share their perspectives on community policing.

Detroit's Fifth Precinct was the first to implement the program. An estimated 200 officers and nine out of 12 precincts participated in the program during its first year, including 40 officers from Detroit's Fifth precinct.

"This interaction allows you to have a voice that will not be adjudicated in a court system, but happen by a conversation," Commander Ewing said. "This is a prime time for all the stuff bottled inside of you to get out. But the first thing you've got to be able to do is to listen and give the other person a voice."

Listening to others, particularly people wearing a police uniform, challenged me. I cringed while hearing officers share stories about working at a job that brings continual risk because in my experience, they cause more harm than they prevent.

Commander Ewing credits the police department's commitment to transparency and the restorative practices he seeded for preventing the rupture of trust in Minneapolis, Ferguson, and Baltimore, where unarmed Black men died at the hands of police officers.

"Imagine being out there on a traffic stop not knowing what you're going to meet when you approach a car," Commander Ewing said. "You have to have some sense of control when you're out there because things can turn on a dime."

But is it possible to expect people who have never experienced justice to trust restorative practices?

Learning to Listen

We fanned to assigned tables around the room after Commander Ewing outlined the day's events.

"Ewing, with his smooth-talking self, think he's slick," an older woman huffed, as we sat down for our small-group, restorative circle.

"If I had known he was going to keep us here all day, I wouldn't have come in the first place," she said. "Does it really take all day to say, 'stop killing our kids?'"

"Mmmm-hmm," another woman chimed in. "I know that's right."

"I have to pick up my grandson this afternoon and start cooking for tomorrow," the older woman continued. "I don't have time to sit in a circle. Why can't we come here, say what we got to say, and leave?"

"What I got to say will take a little longer," said a pastor who joined the group. "This officer gave me a ticket two weeks ago for running a red light. That light was yellow."

Silence shadowed the table as the officer, mentioned earlier, sat down. He and another officer welcomed us to the summit and began asking a series of scripted, restorative practices questions.

"I didn't come here to answer questions," the older woman interrupted. "I came here to tell you to stop killing our boys. You run around these streets like you own them. But you don't. We do. These are our streets."

She stood up, draped her purse around her shoulder like a soldier arming for battle, and headed for the door. But first, she stopped at the buffet table and wrapped three doughnuts and two pastries in a napkin before sweeping out of the room.

The officer chuckled softly and re-read the first five questions, inviting residents to share their worst experiences with police officers and how it made them feel. I squirmed in my seat. I hadn't told my mother what had happened to me until 25 years later. I tucked away her hurt, anger, and disbelief in the handkerchief of my soul. There was no use in airing my trauma out in front of strangers.

We stared at each other politely, waiting for someone to speak up. When no one did, the officer recounted the night he answered a dispatch call to help a woman being beaten and choked by her boyfriend.

The officer spoke with the woman after they detained her boyfriend. She promised the officer she would leave the relationship and rebuild her life. The officer promised to check on her regularly in the following weeks.

"I was riding down the street, and something in my spirit said, 'go check on her,'" the officer explained. "I raced to her house, and when I got there, people were standing outside. They said the boyfriend had come back. I called for backup. I went upstairs and found him straddled over her, choking her. Her six-year-old son was in the corner watching this like it was something on TV."

The officer's voice faltered as he continued, "He went to jail, and she went to the hospital. But she…she didn't make it. Her heart couldn't take the stress he put her through."

"During the investigation, we found out that he poured gasoline all over the house," the officer continued. "After he killed her, he was going to set the house on fire with him and the kids in it. If I hadn't kept my word to check on her…"

The unspoken horror hung between us. I stretched my hand across the table to put over the officer's hand. But instead, I reached for a packet of sugar.

Having My Say

We soberly returned to the main circle 30 minutes later. A representative from each group shared what they learned from the discussion. Residents who were once angry at officers for what they thought were wrongly issued tickets said they were stunned to realize the dangers officers faced each day.

"Wait, what?" I thought. "Since when did police officers get to be the victims? Today, they are dressed in jeans and t-shirts like normal people. Tomorrow, they'll be back in uniforms and carrying guns for another round of state-sanctioned violence."

I empathized with the officer's harrowing story. But I wasn't prepared to see his humanity. So before visiting Detroit, I researched the city's pockmarked history of militarized policing of Black neighborhoods.

During the 1940s and 1950s, Detroit city leaders recruited white, male police officers from southern towns through advertisements in local newspapers because white southerners were experienced in taming and breaking the spirits of Black people. The racial tension sparked the Detroit riots in 1967 that resulted in the deaths of 33 Black people, 7,000 arrests, and 1,000 burned buildings.

Narrowing the political to the personal, I hated police officers because they reminded me of my shame. They were supposed to protect me. But the person who violated me was one of their own. I jumped up from my seat when it was our turn to share the group's discussion.

"You have power because we, the public, give it to you," I said.

I glared at the officers in the room. "My power was taken away from me 25 years ago. Not by one of you. I'm not even from here. I'm just a writer on assignment. He didn't just take away my power; he destroyed my trust in people. If you want my sympathy, you need to earn my trust."

I shook as I sat down. A woman in my group hugged me. Commander Ewing strode over to me.

"I don't know what happened to you," Commander Ewing said. "But you're right. We're trying to make these streets safe, and we have to abide by the trust that has been put into us. And if that trust has been broken, we have to mend that."

Commander Ewing's words partially acknowledged my trauma. But it wasn't enough, because the man who violated me also snatched my innocence. For decades, I lived with a gaping wound. Could restorative practices help me learn to heal my wounds?

Cracking Open

Through a series of interconnected role-playing exercises and group discussions that afternoon, we learned more about the dangers officers face in the line of duty. In turn, they learned about how the public perceives them.

One of the most illuminating moments happened with the police officer who spoke in our small group. I was surprised to learn that he offended most of the citizens participating in the summit. Residents complained about his arrogance and brusque, by-the-book demeanor during traffic stops.

"That light was yellow," the pastor pleaded to the larger group.

The officer slumped further in the chair with each accusation—first from residents, then by co-workers who counseled how he could have better handled the situation. He clenched and unclenched his jaw. Suddenly, I understood.

"I don't know this officer," I said. "I never met him before today."

"Consider yourself lucky," a woman snorted.

I briefly recounted the story the officer told us about the abused woman.

"You may have experienced him as mean or arrogant," I said. "But that's not what this is about. He blames himself for the woman's death. The memory of it imprisons him. He thinks he didn't get there fast enough. Now, he will catch everything before it

occurs, even if it means stopping the pastor here at a 'yellow' light."
I looked at the officer. He nodded and smiled. I smiled back.

Wisdom Without the Fortune Cookie

The remainder of the summit flashed in a haze. I hadn't understood the totality of what happened at the summit until later. I recapped the day's events on the phone with Ted, while waiting for my dinner order at P.F. Chang's. Dishes clanged, and chatter hovered around me. I then realized that injustice never happens in a vacuum. Thousands of broken places contribute to its mosaic—fear, sadness, rage, pain, regret, and shame. Yet, the light also shines through those broken places.

"I don't think I can forgive my abuser," I nearly yelled through the dinner din.

"Restorative practices aren't necessarily about forgiveness," Ted said.

"I forgive myself," I said. Tears dropped from my cheeks and onto the white tablecloth. I sighed. "And that's enough for today."

"That's enough for today," Ted echoed. I could hear the crackle in his voice. He sometimes gets teary when a truth hits him so hard that it shatters his understanding and pieces it back together again.

"Keep me posted," Ted said.

"I will," I said.

Restorative practices provide a path forward that leads with an open heart. If it could help heal decades of shame when all else failed, maybe it was worth investigating. So I dedicated myself to this assignment, learning as much as I could about restorative practices and its power to repair harm, restore relationships, and build social capital.

Just then, the Mongolian beef and rice dish arrived at my table. I picked up the fork and knife. Maybe I will give restorative practices a chance. I said aloud to no one in particular, "Alright, I'm in."

Personal stories are powerful when they inspire collective action. It's gratifying that restorative practices helped me to forgive myself in the aftermath of systemic trauma. However, we have to do more than nod our heads in sympathy when such stories are told. That's why I lean into the concept of restorative communities for answers and action. One facet of a restorative community often informs another. In this concluding essay in the Justice section, I propose that ordinary citizens be given the power to redefine policing for our beleaguered communities in America.—KB

Why It's Time for a Citizens' Assembly on Policing

Wanton endangerment.

That was the verdict a Louisville, Kentucky, grand jury recently gave a police officer in the shooting death of Breonna Taylor. Taylor, a Black woman and emergency room technician, was sleeping when three officers barged into her apartment in March 2020. Serving a "no-knock warrant" that allowed them to enter, the officers fired 32 shots, killing Taylor.

Her death has been a rallying cry against police brutality and racism in the United States. The case captured the covers of *O (Oprah) Magazine* and *Vanity Fair*. Yet only one of the three officers was indicted in Taylor's death. The indictment was not for Taylor's death, but for endangering her neighbors with his shots. Her family received a $12 million settlement. But no amount of money can bring her back.

This was no isolated case. There were 1,055 fatal police shootings in 2021 and 1,021 in 2020. Moreover, the rate of fatal police shootings among Black Americans was much higher than that for any other ethnicities, standing at 38 fatal shootings per million of the population.

It's time for a citizens' assembly on community policing.

A Historic Problem

Modern policing in the United States began in the 1830s. Northern and southern police departments began with different approaches but ultimately arrived at the same place by the 1950s, according to Dr. Gary Potter, a Criminal Justice professor and researcher at Eastern Kentucky University's Police Studies program.

Northern cities created formal police organizations when "watchmen" and volunteers proved unreliable by getting drunk or falling asleep on the job. Professional police organizations sprang up in Boston (the first in 1838), New York City (1845), Chicago (1851), and Philadelphia (1855). Police officers were publicly supported, full-time employees with continuous employment. Departments had permanent, fixed rules and procedures. They were accountable to a central governmental authority.

Southern policing was an outgrowth of "slave patrols" created in the Carolina counties in 1704. Slave patrols chased, captured, and returned enslaved Blacks to plantation owners. They also terrorized, punished, and lynched Blacks to discourage revolts, and as a form of vigilante justice for perceived offenses.

Following the Civil War, the slave patrols morphed into police departments deployed to control newly "freed" Blacks now working as sharecroppers in a cruel, agricultural caste system. Southern police also enforced "Jim Crow" segregation laws, established to deny Blacks access to human and voting rights.

An amalgamation of northern and southern policing models developed to respond to six million Blacks' movement from the rural South to urban cities in the Northeast, Midwest, and West between 1916 and 1970, known as the "Great Migration." For example, midwestern cities such as Detroit recruited police officers from the South because they knew how to "handle" Blacks.

Public outcry after decades of corruption led to a series of reforms in the 1950s. However, in decades to come, additional bureaucracy and an emphasis on military-style organizational discipline in police departments lit the fuse for militarized policing in Black and brown communities.

Middle-Class Flight and the Illusion of Safety

Until recently, most people have responded to police brutality by not responding to it.

They perceive police brutality as an "earned" response to an alleged crime. As neighborhood demographics change, many people flee to "safer" neighborhoods. They assume the police will contain such problems to the now Black and brown communities they left behind.

But as we've seen from the ongoing racial protests following the deaths of Breonna Taylor and George Floyd, militarized policing is a public safety threat and should be treated as such. We cannot leave matters of policing to politicians who receive support and protection from unions and other special interests. We must remember and invoke that elected officials and the police departments they fund serve the citizens, not the other way around. This is why a citizens' assembly on the issue is vital to changing the culture of policing in the United States.

There are many reasons ordinary citizens can make thoughtful decisions on complex issues. Among the top two are that citizens are more collaborative and willing to change their minds than legislators. They don't have to run for re-election or answer to special interests for campaign contributions. Citizens' assemblies can bring America together again, and you can try them without changing the federal or state Constitution.

An Enlightened Revolution

Citizens need to talk to and not at each other. A conversation about race and the role and future of policing must happen in

American communities without the influence or interference of politicians, police unions, activist groups, or the media.

Instead, ordinary people need to gather (virtually or in-person) to discuss racism in policing, the right of the safety of all human beings, the weaponization of safety against marginalized groups, and the elements it takes to establish and maintain a fair and just society.

A new policing model could emerge from these conversations that respects fundamental human rights, drastically decreases police shootings, keeps communities safe, and ensures an appropriate response to behavioral health issues. We must also denounce hate crimes and white supremacy masquerading as vigilante justice.

Coupled with the reforms proffered by the Black Lives Matter movement, the NAACP, and other social justice groups, a citizens' assembly on policing demolishes the notion of "law and order" and replaces it with sustainable, safe communities.

Together, we can spark a revolution through conversation. We aim to repair harm, restore relationships, and build social capital in our communities, with our police, and most importantly, with each other. We must do so because our very lives depend on it.

7

Enterprise

More than 47 million Americans quit their jobs in 2021.

A global pandemic coupled with months of uncertainty in quarantine gave people lots of time to think. Many employees decided they no longer wanted 60-hour work weeks or to chase the myth of work/life balance. So, they quit.

Other factors leading to the "Great Resignation" include wage stagnation coupled with rising living costs, long-lasting job dissatisfaction, workplace safety concerns during COVID, and the desire to work for companies with better remote-working policies.

Companies, as of this writing, are scrambling to keep good employees. Organizations that realize hierarchal management models are becoming increasingly obsolete will be the most successful in hiring and retaining star employees.

Growing evidence suggests that companies achieve better outcomes when employees have more voice, choice, and shared responsibility. "Enterprise" in a restorative community means employees are engaged in decision-making, and business decisions balance profits with effectively and consistently contributing to the social good.

But how do companies achieve such lofty-seeming aims, especially during times of volatility and uncertainty?

Before the pandemic, some organizations, like a nonprofit we'll profile in this section, sought the radical solution of flat management. Eradicating as much hierarchy as possible, a flat management structure has relatively few or no levels of middle management between executives and frontline employees.

Other companies employ check-ins—a simple, yet deceptively powerful, approach that encourages each person in a meeting to speak and be heard by their peers.

This section features Richard Cohen's "Check-In Success" model. In a series of blog posts, Richard, an internationally recognized corporate trainer, shares leadership strategies that further workplace development and ultimately enable it to perform at the highest level.

"Enterprise" in a restorative community is not only for staff meet-ings and performance reviews. We'll visit a Third District Court in Detroit and a small-town newspaper in New Hampshire that employ restorative practices to boost positive community engagement and restore civility in public discourse.

The following section is excerpted from Richard Cohen's website,
www.checkinsuccess.com.—KB

The Power of Check-Ins

By Richard Cohen

I've always been a little obsessed with human contact. Partly, this is because of the work I do. For the past 30 years, I've been a facilitator, trainer, and mediator, specializing in leadership development and conflict resolution. I work with people—in corporations, government agencies, courts, nonprofits, and schools—who want to engage in honest, productive conversations that will move their lives and organizations forward.

It's not unusual for me to assist groups after things have become especially challenging: when people see things very differently, feelings run hot, relationships deteriorate, and the stakes are high.

But the truth is, even under normal circumstances, we tend to be afraid of one another: afraid we'll say something stupid, afraid we'll be excluded, afraid to be ourselves. This is true even in the best organizations and even when we feel we know one another well. And when we feel scared and disconnected, it's simply harder to do what our organizations expect of us:

> adapt and learn
> think creatively
> resolve differences
> and deliver excellent work.

My interest in connection is also personal. My wonderful mother struggled with depression for her entire life. I wasn't aware of it until I grew older, but my early childhood left me with a deep sense of isolation and an equally powerful longing to make contact. For better and worse, my life schooled me in the pain of disconnection, and it motivated me to minimize that pain for others and myself. That's why check-ins became part of my standard operating procedure at work.

The One Practice Too Many Successful Managers Ignore

Check-ins are an approach to encourage each person in a meeting to speak to their peers. Group members respond to a selected question or prompt one by one. Prompts are chosen to elicit who participants are, how they feel, or what they think about an almost limitless range of work-related and personal concerns. Leaders use check-ins deliberately to further a group's development and, ultimately, to enable it to perform at the highest level.

I don't remember when I was first introduced to check-ins.

That isn't surprising, given the practice is as old as humans. Like most of you, I likely participated in my first check-in as a seven-year-old. ("Can everyone go around and share their name and favorite animal?"). I've conducted them or watched colleagues conduct them countless times. We all know about check-ins, right?

Wrong. Over the years, I've been confounded by how many leaders are unfamiliar with the practice of check-ins. More accurately, they are familiar with it—they attended elementary school, too—but they don't incorporate it into their meetings.

I'm not talking about slackers here, either. I'm referring to seasoned, high-performing leaders in some of the world's most successful corporations and nonprofits. Smart people to whom leading meetings are like at-bats to baseball players; they do it multiple times every day, hundreds of times a year. It's a central part of their jobs.

These same leaders express their frustration and disappointment with meetings, particularly the difficulty of engendering the kind of authentic and brave conversation that would make their gatherings most valuable. They complain that a handful of people attending their meetings do most of the talking, and that many employees don't talk at all.

Yet, more often than not, they were neglecting check-ins: one of the simplest, most efficient tools I know for increasing any group's engagement, trust, and productivity.

But simple doesn't mean easy. Most leaders know their business well and expect high performance, but they haven't had much training in how to enable people to work together. And they are even less comfortable with the social-emotional dimension of team performance.

As I paid more attention to check-ins, I noticed that some of my colleagues take them for granted. They forget to apply best practices, and as a result, they don't get the maximum benefit from their check-ins. It became clear to me that people could use some help.

Check-In Success

I searched for books and other resources about check-ins that could guide leaders. There wasn't much—a page or two in one resource, a paragraph or two in another. That was it. Check-ins have been hiding in plain sight. I created the website "Check-In Success" to fill that gap.

Like many things that we think are simple—a raindrop falling, playing catch with a child, a leaf—when you look closely, the underlying structures and processes are more intricate than you would have guessed. The same is true here. Conducting an effective check-in is connected to profound and usually unspoken human needs, to how we communicate, to how we plan and run meetings, and to how we show up in every aspect of our leadership.

I've tried to address these nuances on the website (www. checkinsuccess.com). But zoom out, and check-ins are still quite simple: people gathered together, with each person taking a turn to say a few words to their fellows.

My greatest hope goes out to you and the people with whom you gather. May the "Check-In Success" resource enable you to make your meetings more successful—and enjoyable.

A Culture of Collaboration

As meetings become ever more crucial, so too, do check-ins. Tens of millions of meetings happen every workday around the world. You likely spend about 35 percent of your time in meetings if you're a middle manager. In upper management, meetings probably account for nearly half of your work life.

The contemporary workplace requires us to collaborate more than ever before. We spend 50 percent more time working together than we did two decades ago, often in cross-functional settings. Significantly, almost all decisions of consequence are now made by groups. At Google and similar iconic companies, even decisions that traditionally were made unilaterally by managers—like whom to hire, fire, and promote—are made by teams.

Leveraging the Power of Teams

But to leverage the many advantages of working in groups—faster innovation, higher job satisfaction, and better results—group members have to *work well together.*

And this is not easy to do. Human beings are complex. Many leaders have treated meeting participants as gears in a machine, able to perform at a high level just by being assembled in the same location. It's no wonder they report that most of their meetings are failures.

Experienced facilitators have long understood the power and importance of check-ins. Today there is a growing appreciation and increasing evidence for why this straightforward practice improves group performance.

Check-Ins Make Groups (Work) Smarter

Recent research has demonstrated that groups, like individual people, have characteristic levels of intelligence. The intelligence level of any group can predict its performance on a wide variety of tasks.

Surprisingly, the top indicators of so-called "collective intelligence" do not concern who group members are—their average individual intelligence, motivation level, or degree of extroversion—but rather *how group members behave*. Chief among the behaviors that predict a group's intelligence is whether group members talk roughly the same amount of time, what researchers call "the equality of conversational turn-taking."

Check-ins prime a group for just that: Their structure explicitly encourages group members to talk in roughly equal measure. Check-ins get everyone to participate right at the start, including those who might hesitate to speak for various reasons. After people speak once, they are more likely to participate again.

The power of check-ins so impressed researchers at Johns Hopkins University that they called the process the "activation phenomenon." Their study of surgical teams found that when members introduced themselves and shared concerns before they operated, the average number of complications and deaths fell by 35 percent.

When group members are comfortable speaking, they take responsibility for problems, share their insights, and most efficiently generate solutions. By getting all members to use their voice, check-ins make groups smarter.

Check-ins Help Groups Focus and Align

Think about it: Whenever a meeting begins, each group member has to transition from whatever they were doing before to whatever is about to happen in your gathering.

Whether they were writing a report, working on a shop floor, helping a customer, or thinking about their kids, everyone has been focused on something else.

Check-ins function like the tuning of an orchestra. Before musicians collaborate, we all know that they take a few minutes to tune their instruments to a standard pitch. This enables them to work together in harmony. Check-ins are a kind of tuning that facilitates social rather than musical interaction.

When used skillfully, check-ins guide members to pause, put aside what came before, and focus on what they hope to accomplish together. Check-ins mark a boundary between outside and inside the meeting. They separate past and present while engaging, aligning, and inspiring.

Check-Ins Help Create Psychological Safety

Whether we are aware of it or not, and particularly at the start of relationships and events, we are all instinctively concerned with what others think of us and ask unspoken questions like:

> Am I safe?
> Am I included?
> Am I respected and valued?

We can't devote our full energies to anything else until we can answer these fundamental questions in the affirmative. When we can—when we do feel relatively secure, included, and valued—we have what has come to be called psychological safety: "a climate characterized by interpersonal trust and mutual respect, in which people are comfortable being themselves."

Check-ins implicitly address these primary human concerns before many realize we have them. Because each person's input is solicited and implicitly appreciated, check-ins make group members feel welcome, valued, and connected.

It's as though, through their check-in, each group member says, "I am here," and the group, attending to them, in essence, responds, "We see you."

Done regularly and well, check-ins become rituals that deepen our feelings of safety and belonging. Moreover, they inspire us to devote more of our resources to the task.

Check-Ins Strengthen Relationships

Strong relationships lead to strong performance.

By definition, strong relationships have a high degree of trust—the "firm belief in the reliability, truth, ability, or strength of someone." When group members trust each other, behaviors that are critical to collaboration become possible:

> We challenge one another.
> We give others the benefit of the doubt.
> We strive to understand differing perspectives.
> We speak up.
> We risk engaging in the kind of constructive disagreement necessary to reach optimal solutions.

Done well, check-ins are elegant and efficient trust-generators. They intentionally encourage openness and vulnerability. When groups of people first meet, simply hearing one another's voices reduces our animal vigilance and begins to build trust. Group members learn about each other and form personal connections ("Oh, I didn't know you grew up in the Midwest, like cooking, feel the same way I do about that issue, etc.").

Perhaps most importantly, check-ins intentionally encourage openness and vulnerability.

Strong relationships are an asset for any human endeavor, the foundation for high performance. Check-ins work to create and strengthen that foundation.

Check-Ins Reveal What Is True

Check-ins tap into people's craving for authenticity and the feelings of connection and ease that can accompany it.

They initiate a positive feedback cycle driven by the human urge to connect, something I call the "unwinding" of a group. Here's how it works: One person testing the waters takes a small risk in their check-in remarks. A subsequent member, feeling emboldened by that earlier speaker (and the group's accepting response), shares something even more revelatory.

Gradually, people up the ante until the group is more willing to speak truthfully than they were at the start, often dramatically so. As a result, we can achieve an uncommon level of honesty and intimacy in a single check-in, and it can deepen over the life of a group.

Ultimately, this honesty and courage serve any endeavor. It makes group members more likely to challenge one another, admit mistakes, share thoughts or experiences that don't align with official policy, and offer untested but potentially breakthrough ideas. Done well, check-ins send groups on a path toward their unique truth, where people can communicate more authentically and apply more of their collective resources to any challenge.

What is particularly satisfying is that this culture of openness is generated by the group itself. Though the check-in provides an enabling context, it is group members' own behaviors—in the form of individual risks taken, and the rewarding of those risks—that creates the openness. It is truly theirs.

Done well, check-ins send groups on a path toward their own unique truth, where people can communicate more authentically and apply more of their collective resources to any challenge.

Check-Ins Generate Energy and Enjoyment

When check-ins work, people lean in to listen.

Whether the question is lighthearted or profound, we want to hear how our fellows will respond. We are engaged. Check-ins also enable group members to form closer, more vital relationships. Such groups aren't the norm for most of us. We like going to groups where we feel we belong; it feels good to see and be seen.

And what about fun!? Check-ins produce more than their share of positive feelings. These emotions are contagious, traveling fast in a group under the right circumstances. Enjoyment also has corollaries like trust, passion, and commitment that can inspire groups to produce better work.

Laughter, in particular, is a powerful bonding force. Research has demonstrated that couples who laugh together have more successful, longer-lasting relationships, which is likely true of people in other groups. So, I always feel that a group is making progress if they laugh together.

Successful check-ins grab people's attention and connect them. By doing so, they establish a norm of high energy and high participation. And once engaged, people are more inclined to focus for the rest of the meeting (even if the content is not as engrossing).

Check-Ins Help Groups Learn

Check-ins increase learning by providing access to one of the most powerful resources available: the wisdom of the group.

They tap a group's collective insight into the substantive issues they face and shed light on what matters most to any group. A strength of check-ins is that you don't only hear from the usual suspects: their egalitarian structure means everyone contributes, even the quieter members.

Countless times, I've witnessed groups' surprise when a more reserved member—who otherwise might not have spoken—makes an uncommonly insightful contribution. In this way, check-ins can provide a more comprehensive accounting of what a group knows than might be ascertained by merely posing a question to the entire group.

What you learn from group members' insights and experiences can inform course corrections on any initiative and even lead to modifications of the format or focus of the meeting itself. Groups often have greater resources and the ability to address their challenges than we think. By enabling group members to learn from one another, check-ins help unleash that potential.

Check-Ins Are an Essential Practice

It can seem counterintuitive, but to enable groups to do their best work, we need to reserve time to enable them to step back, hear all voices, come to know one another, and even explore topics only tangentially related to their core purpose.

Check-ins generate powerful resources—greater trust, sharper focus, stronger relationships, deeper insights—which help groups navigate the inevitable challenges of collaboration and perform at the highest level.

Certainly, check-ins are not the only tool you can use to make meetings great. They are, however, one of the easiest, quickest—you can do one in literally 15 seconds per person!—and most fundamental. Plus, when check-ins are conducted skillfully, they make people feel good.

At the risk of mixing tool metaphors, consider this: Check-ins are to leading groups what hammers are to building houses. Of course, you couldn't build a house with a hammer alone, but it would be very hard to build one without one. So too, are check ins for countless leaders, for all the reasons detailed above.

Richard Cohen is the founder of Great Ponds Resolutions. He enables individuals, teams, and organizations to increase their influence, collaborate effectively, manage workplace conflict, and be more successful. For more information, visit greatpondresolutions.com.

Working Without a Boss

What if you went to work tomorrow and there was no boss? What if there was no one person to set the vision and mission of the company and assign duties accordingly? What if there wasn't one person who measured your performance and determined your pay based on how well you met the boss's quarterly objectives? What if you could choose the job responsibilities you liked, rather than straining to conform to the dictates of a job description?

Ligand, a restorative practices training organization in Kortrijk, Belgium, is building such a reality.

Reinventing an Organization

A self-described "soulful" organization, Ligand began a decade ago as a two-person team dedicated to employing "recovery-oriented" and "positive reorientation" approaches to addressing urgent challenges facing children, families, and communities in West Flanders.

While Ligand remains devoted to its core mission, its staff and scope of work have significantly expanded in recent years. Rather than gather in a conference room to devise solutions on a white-board, Ligand staffers began discussing the idea of flattening their organization two years ago. Team members were influenced by Frederic Laloux's management classic Reinventing Organizations and wanted to integrate principles that enabled the practice of "self-management" or "self-steering" at Ligand.

Together-management operates through an interdependent network of autonomous teams. There is no hierarchy and job descriptions, job titles, or bosses. Decision-making is highly distributed among the group. Everyone is given access to all information at the same time. Disagreements are resolved among peers by using a well-defined conflict resolution process. Peers hold each other accountable to shared commitments.

Self-management takes the principle of the restorative practice that "people are happier and more likely to make positive changes when those in authority do things with rather than to or for them" by abolishing authority.

"When you have one leader, it makes the organization vulnerable," said Sabine Bourgeois, director of Oranjehuis, a Ligand affiliate that uses restorative practices to help children and families in crisis. "It's hard to have one leader and not have it be an obstacle for the organization to grow and develop."

A Restless Leader

All this talk about self-management made Stijn Deprez, Ligand's coordinator (executive director), restless.

"I started questioning myself," Stijn said. "Is my current role still something for me? I haven't got the talent for administrative chores, and I have to admit I don't like them. But, on the other hand, I am someone who enjoys developing and carrying out new ideas."

Stijn also noticed that a team leader's patterns often influence the team. For example, he questioned whether his self-defined pattern of believing everything would "end up well" prevented the team from facing its challenges.

The Ligand team discussed Stijn's concerns during a teambuilding retreat, which was illuminated by the light and heat of a campfire on the Belgian coast. Some staffers thought Stijn's proposal was an excuse to leave the organization. Some team members voiced regret and guilt. Others expressed gratitude and praised Stijn for his courage. The group refrained from pressing toward solutions until everyone had a chance to speak and be heard. Then, each member of Ligand's staff engaged in the annual ritual of burning their employment contract in the fire.

"We traditionally make a clear choice to sign a new contract at the beginning of each work year," Stijn said. "That way, we can begin each year with intention. We know that our job is not all roses and moonlight, and we accept that. Instead of lamenting that, we make a clear choice to come back and experience the joy of our first day of work."

A New Reality at Ligand

Together, the Ligand team decided to take the bold and innovative step of eliminating Stijn's position as coordinator and flattening the organization.

After discussing Ligand's mission, vision, and values, the group divvied up the organization's administrative duties and roles on separate pieces of paper and passed them around the circle. If someone wanted to assume one of Stijn's former duties, they held on to the piece of paper. Now, every team member is responsible for specific tasks or partial tasks.

Ligand's roles are now defined as "inspirer," "communicator," "decision-maker," "culture conservator," "administrator," and "connector."

"When you are given a certain role, this does not mean you will be the only one who will perform the task," Stijn explained. "It does mean that you have to ensure that eventually the task is brought to an end."

The decision to flatten Ligand's organizational structure raised doubts and concerns. However, team members discuss concerns and devise solutions together. Implemented in October [2019], Ligand will try the new organizational structure for a year [the experiment has continued]. One of the biggest challenges is helping people outside the organization know who to turn to for help and questions.

"We are confident that our new approach will work," Stijn said. "Of course, we will keep a finger on the pulse. We have many moments of consultation, and we adjust things whenever necessary."

In the meantime, Stijn uses his free time, now that he is no longer Ligand's coordinator, to experiment with a new productivity tool—doing nothing.

"Apparently doing nothing improves our creativity and problem-solving," said Stijn, whose new role at Ligand involves maintaining the company's culture, inspiring others, and external communications. "It may sound strange but doing nothing makes us more productive. Sounds like a great idea to me."

Where Are They Now?

Ligand's nimble organizational model allowed Stijn to put his talents to good use during the pandemic.

He wrote three books and developed online training programs, for example. A new online platform improves Ligand's effectiveness while training more participants in restorative practices.

In addition, they look for ways to meet as smaller teams to go for a walk or sit outside to discuss an issue rather than gather in a building.

"I'm more convinced that the better your connections and relationships, the more resilient you are in coping with challenges," Stijn said. "Right now, it's COVID. Maybe next year it's something else. The more connected you are, the stronger you are."

Can Better Workplaces Make Detroit a Better City?

The dried spit on the customer service window at the end of the workday was a telltale sign that things needed to change at Michigan's Third Judicial Circuit Court in Detroit.

"It was on both sides, too," explained Zenell Brown, the court's executive administrator. "They are yelling at you, and you are yelling at them. There was no (positive) connection between the citizens and the (frontline) staff."

Two Tales, One City

Detroit has been an American emblem of urban violence, crime, and poverty for decades.

Michigan state lawmakers made several efforts to "revitalize" Detroit. First, they appointed a series of emergency managers and a "reform" mayor, who have helped Detroit move out of bankruptcy, board up abandoned houses, and restore city services.

However, there is an untold story about the growing commitment among neighborhood and nonprofit leaders, teachers, parents, and frontline city employees to change the culture of Detroit from the inside. They are not waiting for sweeping governmental reforms to restore peace, civility, and economic prosperity in their city. Instead, residents are learning and implementing restorative practices to build social capital and achieve social discipline through participatory learning and decision-making.

"I now have hope that we can migrate toward communicating and functioning better at work," said Benita Cheatom, Brown's colleague and Executive Director of Human Resources and Labor Relations at the Third Judicial Court of Michigan. "Once we respect and understand each other as colleagues, we can extend it to the entire community."

Restoring Workplaces and Communities

Cheatom and Brown say they are already noticing a significant difference among the court supervisors and managers who have undergone restorative practices training.

Restorative practices create a safe space where participants can resolve issues, encourage thoughtful dialogue, and connect people to their feelings. Engaging in restorative circles, for example, has improved workplace communication. Circles are a versatile restorative practice, enabling employees to tell their stories and offer their perspectives as an alternative to formal, hierarchical meetings that rely on win-lose positioning and argument.

"Restorative practices help us see each other as humans," Cheatom said. "We learn to overcome our differences and begin to understand how alike we are."

Sustaining Restorative Practices in the Future

Michigan's Third Judicial Circuit Court is just one of several public and nonprofit sector organizations gradually implementing restorative practices through its employee ranks.

Schools, local police departments, and social service organizations are also training their staff to use restorative practices.

"We're in the business of changing lives through various programs and services," said Sheilah Clay, then-President and CEO of the Neighborhood Service Organization. It is a nonprofit agency that provides behavioral health, employment, and supportive housing services for children, youth, adults, and older adults in Detroit.

"We know people come to us because something is not going well in their lives," Clay said. "Our job is to help them find their voice. We fix it with them, not for them."

Clay employs restorative practices internally and externally. She used the restorative circle, for example, to help one of her teams deal with the emotional fallout from the departure of one manager and acclimate to a new one. She also wants to use restorative practices in the housing program, to help tenants handle conflicts with the landlord.

"Restorative practices changes how you think," she said. "It changes you so that you avoid these problems in the future. If you can change your attitude and lifestyle, you can change the whole community."

Overcoming Challenges

Implementing restorative practices is not without its challenges.

Employees come and go, for example. As soon as one group is trained, members move on to other opportunities, and new employees join the team. Changing organizational protocols and individual mindsets can also be initially tricky. Finally, getting people to understand how their actions and behaviors contribute to the conflict can be problematic for some people to embrace.

Nevertheless, this is the kind of wholesale change that Clay, Brown, Cheatom, and others who live and work in Detroit want for the future of their city.

"Instead of people picking up weapons and hurting each other, we could talk to each other," Cheatom said. "We have to figure out how to deal with conflict and hurt feelings without it destroying us. We've got to do it, or we won't save our community."

How a Small-Town Newspaper Is Bringing Civility Back to Public Discourse

What if the mainstream media were part of the solution?

That was a soul-searching question asked by Adam Hirshan and Julie Hirshan Hart, the publisher and digital editor of *The Laconia Daily Sun*. Nestled in New Hampshire's Lake Region, the free daily newspaper has a print circulation of 18,000. Its e-Edition boasts more than 1.5 million page views.

"We believe everyone should have access to the news and all of the information they need," Julie said. "We are the only print, daily newspaper in our area. We are relied upon by people to get their news."

A hallmark of *The Laconia Daily Sun* is its practice, dating back to its founding 20 years ago, of publishing almost every letter to the editor it receives.

"We have increasingly been attempting to foster an environment where people feel comfortable sharing their ideas and perspectives about local issues and problems," Julie said. "The newspaper, especially during COVID, is attempting to provide a place where people who may know each other in the community can still come together and exchange ideas."

But the sharp political and social differences that revealed the growing fissures in America's democracy were also corroding the newspaper's opinion pages.

"We felt the tone and the substance of our letters were going away from building a consensus, finding common ground for community issues," Adam said. "It was disheartening. It was also not serving our purpose as a community newspaper anymore."

How We Got Here

How we got to the current level of uncivil discourse is a complex stew of technology, capitalism, media, and society.

"To me, it reflects the unhealthy civil discourse resulting from the reliance on social media instead of traditional news sources," Adam said. "People aren't getting the objective facts. They are being fed information that reinforces their own beliefs by a business that wants them to click as many times (as possible) to see the information they want to believe."

Adam contends that tech companies like Facebook sow the seeds of discord to benefit their shareholders, by using their algorithms to control the flow of accurate news sources the public sees on their feeds. In addition, cable news channels broadcast stories according to the partisan beliefs of their viewers, rather than being a place of consensus and discussion. Adam likens the destructive effects of these practices to the harm tobacco and opioid companies caused by not warning the public about using their products.

The war of words found a new battleground on *The Laconia Daily Sun's* letters-to-the-editor page. Letter writers addressed each other on national, partisan topics rather than providing perspectives on local issues that needed the community's time and attention. Some letter writers resorted to personal and *ad hominem* attacks on each other.

"The letters section became a talk radio station instead of an open forum," Adam said. "We felt an urgency to do something about it."

Returning to Civility

Newsroom leaders partnered with the Endowment for Health to explore the impact of civil discourse on community health.

They applied for and received a grant from the nonprofit to hire a new reporter, whose sole focus was to explore how diverse groups and organizations within their community approached critical, local issues and offered solutions. Through the Endowment for Health, Hart and Hirshan teamed up with the Solutions Journalism Network, which trained the staff in the method and practices of solutions journalism. The training shifted interviewing techniques from capturing information to active listening, called "looping."

Meanwhile, two of its most vigorous, frequent, and opposing letter writers decided to meet for lunch.

"The pair sat down over lunch one day to hear each other out, then co-wrote a letter sharing what they found when they focused on listening, instead of trying to change each other's mind," Hart wrote in an article for the American Press Institute. "Encouraged by the civility we'd seen when the writers came out from behind their names on a page and had a discussion face-to-face, we modeled an event after their lunch meeting."

Forum Panelists

The editorial staff conducted two "tolerance forums" on Zoom, where community leaders and people throughout the community who care about promoting and maintaining civil discourse could gather and exchange ideas.

"We're in the midst of launching a digital town square, where we hope to continue some of the discussions that were started on the panels between ordinary citizens," Julie said.

"We're starting with the people who attended the forums and some of our letter writers, to give them a controlled environment where they are encouraged to be respectful," she continued. "They can go back-and-forth freely, to try to get to the root of someone else's idea and maybe understand it better."

Finally, newsroom leaders changed their editorial policy. Instead of erring on the side of printing every letter submitted, preference is given to letters addressing local topics. In addition, the word limit has contracted from 1,000 to 500 words. Finally, a letter writer can submit one letter per week, which must be addressed to the editor rather than to another letter writer.

"We will never be 'done' learning what it means to learn from one another, be more tolerant of one another," Julie said. "We need everyone's buy-in to get it done. In order for it to be a truly respectful conversation, everyone has to be willing to participate respectfully."

As a veteran journalist of 40 years, Adam says the continuing existence of daily newspapers, which are shrinking in America, is vital to a healthy democracy.

"I still see the value of being the community's daily newspaper," he said. "We can disagree. We can close our ears and not listen to each other. But the views being addressed in a central square, a daily newspaper—that gives me hope."

8

Spirit

Spirit often represents the highest aspirations of humankind.

It is often associated with religion or spirituality. However, "spirit" in a restorative community is the underlying motivation for a new reality that honors the worth of all human beings, and infuses democracy into everyday life.

The following section highlights the work of three exceptional people I met along my restorative journey—Govert van Ginkel, Keisha Allen, and Henry McClendon.

Govert van Ginkel is a trainer, author, motivational speaker, mediator, and executive coach. We first met at an IIRP conference in Kortrijk and again in Amsterdam, to discuss a program to promote restorative practices among business and professional leaders. In an essay especially written for this book, Govert reflects upon a fundamental asset in building a restorative community—the right mindset.

A restorative mindset, as we'll soon learn, is a way of consciousness and being that allows us to invest in our relationships with everything around us. It allows us to dare to hope, dream, and make constructive changes for a better tomorrow.

Based in Detroit, Keisha Allen is nationally recognized among her peers as a phenomenal restorative practices trainer. We met during my interviews with Hope Academy Charter School. I admire her intelligence, kindness, and generous way of seeing the world. In a series of conversations, first published as blog posts, Keisha challenges us to "create brave spaces for brave conversations" and to remember that the most restorative relationship we can have is with yourself.

Finally, we end this section and the book with a profile of Henry McClendon. Henry is the Director of Community Engagement for IIRP and a local pastor and community leader. He was the first person I met in Detroit. His journey to restorative practices is unforgettable and it's an honor to share it with you.

Govert, Keisha, and Henry provide a different perspective about building and sustaining restorative communities. Most restorative practices work is outer focused—reduce suspension and expulsion rates, foster collaboration at work, etc.

However, they invite us to draw inward. Their work invokes the adage,"If you want to change the world, you must first begin with yourself."

Investing in Relationships:
A Restorative Mindset

By Govert van Ginkel

In the book *Emotional Intelligence*, author Daniel Goleman says that our mindset—the way we see the world and process information—stimulates our feelings and determines our actions.

The more we become aware of and understand our thoughts and feelings, the more we will be able to respond empathetically to the thoughts and feelings of others. Our mindset is the lens through which we see the world, which explains our actions. Understanding this means that when we see the negative effects of our actions, we need to question the mindset that created them.

But this is not what we learn in school. In school, we learn to defend our mindset; we debate why we are right, and others are wrong. Questioning our mindset is not valued unless you are interested in meditation and mindfulness. Yet we could all benefit more when we understand that we do not have to identify with our mindset.

Determining Our Mindset

It is not our mindset that determines who we are, but it can determine what we become: happy or angry. Our mindset is structuring our thoughts, including certain concepts that we inherited from those who raised and taught us. When we question our thoughts and the concepts we learned, we see that not everything is true. But this does require frequent reflection.

This is especially true when we are confronted with friction in our lives. Our primary survival strategy is to run, defend, or attack when confronted with conflict, but it is less likely to be an effective strategy in our modern lives. Predators no longer hunt us and creating good relationships and talking through our differences will get us better results in everyday life.

Reflecting on our impulsive behavior will help us to see the thoughts and the pattern of the mindset that created our reaction. Healthy contemplation helps us to understand what makes us happy and what does not. Human beings are happy and thrive when they experience feeling connected with others and suffer when they don't. Therefore, we want to restore the connection when it is lost. People all over the world have found different ways to achieve this.

Some traditions are even so old that we nearly have forgotten about them. To our detriment, I would say, because we are not doing that great when it comes to nurturing connection today as a society. Instead, we live in highly individualized societies where we hardly know each other. We, therefore, need to find new ways and a new mindset to restore the connection we so desperately need to function well and overcome our differences.

Overcoming Differences

As a lawyer, I have always been interested in solving conflicts, and it made me look for better ways than the law offers.

Applying the law may lead to a verdict and the idea that justice was done, but it doesn't make people feel or behave better. So, I became highly interested when I came across Restorative Practices more than a decade ago. There are many Restorative Practices, and the aim is always to develop community and manage conflict and tensions by repairing harm and building relationships. It is the opposite of the current punitive system in which we find and punish the wrongdoer and break our relationship. It is the opposite of what we have been doing for centuries.

I was curious if people could change and become better at solving their differences fairly, humanely, and compassionately. It would require changing our minds about how we see ourselves, our relationships, and deal with conflict. What I saw and heard inspired me. I met many fellow travelers on this path to a better way of living together. I also saw that we had not achieved this goal yet, that it was a work in progress. It was a learning process and growing together that we still had to do. It made me wonder about our process, our path. What will bring us together?

Creating a Restorative Mindset

What I also noticed was that certain ways that we think about ourselves and others have become so ingrained over the centuries that we will continue to struggle with conflict if we do not change how we think and behave. Restorative Practices provide a tool that can help us get there, but it needs to grow beyond a tool that we use only when we face problems.

For example, the word restorative seems to focus on repairing a situation, but would it not be better when we do not need any repair because we have found a way to live together harmoniously?

What we need is a Restorative Mindset.

We always will have our differences. How we deal with these differences determines how well we live together. Changing our mindset doesn't mean that we have to agree on everything. I think we will have achieved a Restorative Mindset when we always start by seeing the good in each other and being focused on working together so that everyone is heard and we do our best to make sure all needs are met sustainably.

In a Restorative Mindset, we are ahead of the curve, and the focus is on maintaining good relationships that create community. Restorative Practices will be far less used to repair relationships but instead be used as models that we use to make sure we stay connected and create mutual understanding and decision-making for the solutions that we seek together.

Changing Our Mindset

But how do we change our mindset?

Well, first, we have to become aware of our current mindset. Becoming conscious of the particular way in which you see the world is a start. By doing so, we may discover the values we have and the concepts we believe. Next, I would suggest we question what this means and if what I think and believe is true.

I also wonder what the consequences of seeing reality in this way are. Through this process, I start to understand the changes I can make that will benefit my life and the life of others. This is where the creative process starts. How do I know what a better mindset is? Maybe it starts with asking how we want to live together. Then, a little out-of-the-box dreaming I need to do to envision a better future.

We tend to think about our problems, hoping that we will have achieved our goal when we fix them. But unfortunately, I am afraid this has not worked so far, and all it has done is affirm the status quo. Once we think about problems, we see them every-where, and when one is solved, another appears because of the mindset we inhabit.

We need to dream different and bigger to get something better. Our current mindset becomes just the starting point for a journey to a better destination and to make sure we do not end up with the same thing.

Einstein has been quoted to have said, "We can't solve problems by using the same kind of thinking we used when we created them." We will need something new, a different mindset, to create a way of living together that serves us better. Restorative Practices certainly seem to be a good way to make a start to help us on that journey.

Choosing to "See" Differently

It is important to realize that most of us work and live in an environment where Restorative Practices are sorely needed because we live in a punitive, authoritarian, and paternalistic society.

The consequence of this is that our needs go unmet, making us unhappy. Living in this kind of society also means that unconsciously our mindset is often quite punitive. This becomes clear when we realize how we think about right and wrong, and you hear examples of this in the language we use and our actions.

We forget that words like "conflict" and "problems" are concepts we created. Because we are mostly unaware of how these self-created concepts shape our thinking, we do not realize how we limit our options to find solutions for the needs in our society. It is much harder to find a solution when we have enemy images of each other. Thinking in terms of problems usually leads to right or wrong thinking, which often ends in making people either right or wrong. It creates opposition that makes it much harder to deal with change effectively.

Once we realize that we have a choice to see a situation as either problematic (as a conflict) or as a change of circumstances requiring a new choice, we free our minds to talk with each other without judgment and find mutually satisfying solutions. Life becomes easier when we can freely talk about the changes that happen and discuss how we want to deal with them in a way that benefits us all.

Seeking Solutions

I work with groups and individuals. They often struggle in their lives and want to make a change. A direction that sees new opportunities and is more collaborative in seeking solutions. I use the following steps:

1. I listen to understand the client's reality and the mindset that creates his thoughts and feelings.

2. I help the client become aware of his thoughts, feelings, mindset, and the consequence these have for meeting his needs.

3. We do a reality check and explore the thoughts and concepts that form someone's beliefs to see what is of value, what we want to keep, and what we can let go of.

4. We look at the mindset as one of many lenses we can see to find a more productive one.

5. We determine the practice that can help the client embody the new mindset over time.

6. We define how we will know this goal has been reached and how we will celebrate its achievement.

Finding Sustainable Ways to Live Together

The present system we live in is mainly focused on goals of productivity and economic growth instead of our well-being.

The consequence is that while we desperately need to find better and sustainable ways of living together, the system we live in is not very conducive to Restorative Practices or a restorative way of living. Restorative Practices take a backbench and are only used for the most problematic areas in our society. Because this is so, it only looks at fixing a problem rather than finding a way that integrates all parts of society. It is the consequence of the old mindset of problem thinking.

Instead, we need the opportunity to talk about our needs and become part of the decision-making process so that decisions are not made for us by those that often have different interests at heart.

Each system has its survival as a priority, and this means power structures that favor the few will stay firmly in place. To change this dilemma, we need to shift how we think about ourselves. For example, we need to find new and inclusive ways like we see in citizens' assemblies.

We need to become part of the conversation and together find solutions to most of our needs. This conversation will not only have a generative effect on better outcomes but will also make us better neighbors and partners. It will create a restorative community and way of living, not by having that as a goal, but as the outcome of the process we will have gone through together.

Starting With a Restorative Mindset

It starts with a restorative mindset at the personal and intrapersonal level before we can arrive at a restorative mindset at the community level.

It is the kind of consciousness that I think Gandhi, King, and Mandela held and how they affected others through which it spread. They all faced difficult situations and wondered how to create a better life. They started by questioning their perspectives first. Then, they wondered how they had been part of the problem and which mindset it would take to make a positive change.

They sought to inspire others through their message and so changed the mindset in the society in which they lived. They also chose to stand up for their needs inclusively and cooperatively and hold their ground through nonviolent direct action. They were setting an example we could follow. They didn't ask others to be as determined or disciplined as they were but inspired us by suggesting we take another look at ourselves, question our thoughts and actions, and see a new possibility by seeing others and ourselves in a new light. They were helping us to change our minds and create a new mindset.

A mindset is a habitual way of thinking. A positive mindset is essential to creating sustainable change. Our habits do not change because we see other people with different habits. We change our habit for another because we realize that it serves us better. The same can be said of our mindset. Our mindset serves until we notice that a different mindset will serve us better. Then we change our minds! Others, like Gandhi, King, and Mandela, offered us a mirror we could look into to come to a new insight about ourselves and the world.

Living in Restorative Consciousness

Restorative Practices are a tool, a stepping stone that helps me get into the groove of living restoratively.

It helps me think differently, create new experiences, and find new solutions. Restorative Practices, much like any other idea to create change, be it Restorative Justice, Nonviolent Communication, or something else, is a means to the goal of social change. However, we must remember that any tool we use or system we create is meant to serve our well-being. Therefore, we need to prioritize this and prevent the system from becoming more important than the people it serves.

You need a Restorative Mindset to build a Restorative Community. A Restorative Practice can help create this mindset, but when it is only used as a tool to solve problems, it will have little effect on the way we live our daily lives. For example, you want people to become better neighbors, colleagues, and partners. For that to happen, people have to change their minds, have a change of heart, and see each other in a new light because they come from a restorative perspective in their lives. Live in a restorative consciousness. When we grow beyond using Restorative Practices as a tool, it doesn't matter what we then call it, but it is the answer to the question of how we want to live together.

In this mindset, no matter what we do, we always look for the good in each other, how we can support each other, how we can move on from where we are. When things are difficult, we enter the room thinking about cooperation instead of conflict. This changes how we think, respond to the words we choose and use our posture and tone. In the end, this determines what we can achieve together. That is what I call a restorative way of living. We always are looking for how we can support each other and together create success.

The embodiment of the Restorative Practice moves us into a Restorative Consciousness and creates a new mindset. We need to remember there is a difference between living restoratively as a reality and using restorative practices as a tool for certain circumstances. Our mindset changes and affects all parts of our lives when we choose to live restoratively. We build a new reality when we ask ourselves how we want to live together and how to get there.

Investing in Relationships

This answers how we create a Restorative Mindset at an individual and community level, but how do we create social change in society?

Learning about Restorative Practices is a strategy that will work for people already interested in a restorative way of living. But how about the rest of the people? How do we get everybody involved?

It is my experience that not everyone is interested in Restorative Practices. Well, I also think that people thrive through connection, and everyone needs it in some way. Instead of getting everyone involved in Restorative Practices, we need to aim for what brings us together, what unites us and helps us work together. This can be a social gathering or a goal-oriented gathering. Both will bring us together, help us get to know each other, and exchange views. We can use tools like Restorative Practices to help us find a form that works best for the topic at hand and support us best to develop a restorative mindset without promoting Restorative Practices. The Restorative Mindset then is not the goal but the result of the process we used and shared.

The issue in our society is that we have the most difficult conversations with each other when we are the least equipped for it. We try to solve our problems while we lack the kind of relationship that creates mutual understanding and helps us find a mutually satisfying solution. This makes it nearly impossible to solve anything.

It becomes obvious then that investing in our relationships is a prerequisite to peacefully living and working together.

Govert van Ginkel holds an LL.M. title in Dutch Law. Based in the Netherlands, he is a mediator, Master Practitioner in Neuro-Linguistic Programming, certified IIRP trainer, facilitator for the Alternatives to Violence Project (AVP) and facilitator for Restorative Circles. Govert is a former chairman of The Mankind Project foundation in the Netherlands and a facilitator for Shadow work. He is an accredited peer reviewer for The Netherlands Bar, the professional organization for Dutch lawyers, and the Institute for Mediation and Family and Inheritance Law.

The following is a conversation with Keisha Allen about blending restorative practices with self-care, the importance of "creating brave spaces in restorative communities," and what we can learn from them.

Keisha is a Master Licensed Professional Development Trainer who has led restorative practice training of thousands of organizational leaders, educators, justice practitioners, parents, and youth. She specializes in transforming environments, changing the way we engage and interact with each other, and helping adults shift from punitive to restorative learning environments.—KB

Restorative Self-Care Begins with You

Kerra: What is Restorative Self-Care?

Keisha: Restorative practices aim to build community by managing conflict and tension to repair harm and restore relationships. One of the challenges with this work is that many people see restorative practices as outside of themselves.

During training, I ask, "Where does community begin?" Most people say, "your neighbors" or "your immediate surroundings." But community begins with you. Within you is a community. You are a complex, diverse being within your community.

If you don't take time to build this community, manage conflict and tension, repair harm, and restore the relationship within yourself, it will be difficult to do these things with others. In the training, people are stressed out and overwhelmed. However, they get the opportunity to leave with specific tools to calm their world and impact their world professionally and personally.

Kerra: **How can we use the basic principles of restorative practices in self-care?**

Keisha: We often say in restorative practices that "people are happier, more cooperative and productive, and more likely to make positive changes in their behavior when those in authority do things with them, rather than to or for them."

All principles, like the social discipline window, fair process, and the restorative practices continuum, apply to yourself first. For example, using the social discipline window, are you a punitive person? Are you neglectful or permissive? *[Fair Process is a concept that has helped those in authority understand how they can use restorative practices to make inclusive decisions. See Kim, W., & Mauborgne, R. (1997). Fair Process. Harvard Business Review, January 1.—KB]*

When you become awakened to how you navigate a crisis, you don't have to respond negatively. Instead, you can choose to have a healthy, happy relationship with yourself. You can allow yourself the opportunity to feel whatever it is you're feeling. You're not holding it in and becoming toxic.

You can also use the restorative practices continuum, such as affective statements. "When this happens, I feel…" How did you feel when such and such took place? Offer a solution. Sometimes the only solution is, "I can't do anything about that." And that's okay too. All of these principles apply to self-care.

Kerra: **What is the one thing you think people misunderstand about restorative practices and self-care?**

Keisha: One of the biggest myths people have about restorative practices is that it's a program. It's not. For me, it's not a tool that goes in your toolbelt. Instead, it's a paradigm shift that changes how you think, feel, and communicate with yourself and others.

The biggest misunderstanding about self-care is that people think they are taking care of themselves and not. Dwight Jones, the Detroit Community School executive director, is very stoic and blank-faced. The training allowed him to become more vulnerable. Before the training, he was convinced he was okay. After the training, he realized he had some work to do.

Kerra: **Why did you develop the class?**

Keisha: I found through my training that I knew how to operationalize restorative practices in schools, the justice system, or (with) the police. But I wondered, "how do I do it for myself?" I wanted to provide a deeper dive into what restorative practices look like when it's just dealing with you.

One of the most popular questions I get is, "how do I get my school or workplace to operationalize restorative practices principles?" If people use these principles for themselves, the issues of buy-in and wanting others to sanction restorative practices kind of go away. If the fruit you're producing is good, it makes people want to come to your tree. Buy-in is not convincing someone else; it's about modeling the behavior and making them come to you themselves.

Kerra: **Why do you think this class is needed now?**

Keisha: I have been doing restorative practices training for nine years. I developed this class a year and a half ago. We live in a space where everything is moving so fast. So many people are trying to keep up with this moment.

We forgot to take care of ourselves. It's not even normal to think about taking care of ourselves. Most people don't think about what they need. They live on autopilot. We go to work. We come home. We relax. We go to bed. We wonder why we have stress, anxiety, and depression. We don't take time for us.

This pandemic reminds us of the beauty and value of stopping and taking the time to drink in your family or having some alone time. It's needed because we are in a time of trauma and crisis. If people don't take time for themselves and address their issues, it can overwhelm them.

Creating a Brave Space for Brave Conversations

Kerra: **How do you define a "brave space"?**

Keisha: Safe spaces are where you are trying not to hurt people's feelings. A brave space is not a safe space. In a brave space, we don't necessarily know what will happen. We show up because we are willing to be transparent, authentic, and vulnerable.

Kerra: **What is a "brave conversation"?**

Keisha: A brave conversation derives from the "engagement" piece of the Fair Process in restorative practices and a conversation I had with my dad. "Engagement," in restorative practices, means involving individuals in decisions that affect them by listening to their views and genuinely taking their opinions into account.

When my husband proposed, my father asked me what it meant to be engaged. To be "engaged" means to be willing to enter into war for the promise on the other side.

The downtimes will show you who you are and what your capacity is.

People shy away from brave conversations. When we are doing restorative questions in schools, the students say, "I would rather you suspend me than have this conversation." There is a deeper connection and deeper commitment when you choose to have brave conversations.

Kerra: **What are the elements of a brave conversation?**

Keisha: The elements of a brave conversation are authenticity, vulnerability, openness, mutual respect, and the willingness to show up.

Kerra: **How do you apply the elements of a brave conversation in real life?**

Keisha: When my husband proposed, my father asked me what it means to be "engaged." He said to be "engaged" means to be willing to enter into war for the promise on the other side.

But we also use "engagement" in the "Fair Process" principle of restorative practices. To me, "Fair Process" sums up what it means to create brave spaces for brave conversations. "Fair Process" includes engagement, explanation, and expectation clarity.

"Engagement" encourages everyone's involvement in decision-making. "Explanation" provides participants with an understanding of why decisions are made. "Expectation clarity" requires that everyone should understand the implications of the decision and what it means in the future.

Kerra: What kinds of brave conversations are you currently having on a community level?

Keisha: Conversations between police officers and community residents are one example. Each has a perception of the other, and it drives our perception and not in a good way. These brave conversations can transform what you believe about the other person.

Other brave conversations include those between churches and the gay community, conversations about race and racism, conversations within the Black community, conversations between husbands and wives, and conversations young people have with their parents.

These are brave conversations because we don't feel like we have to control the narrative. But, like water, these conversations will take the shape they need to.

Kerra: What is the bravest conversation you've had in the past six months?

Keisha: It was with me a couple of weeks ago. I was in the hospital. I blacked out and hit my head and face against the wood railing of our bed. I felt stiffness in my body and couldn't move my neck. The pain became so intense it felt like my head was coming off my shoulders.

I went to the hospital. I had to sit there. I had to stop. I asked myself, "What does neck stiffness mean spiritually?" It is the balance between the neck and the heart. I have been sitting at the computer too long and not drinking enough water. I had to say, "Ok, Keisha, you talk about others taking care of themselves. Are you taking care of yourself?

What are the lies you have been telling yourself?" Before I hit my head, I was up until 4 a.m., working, typing away on the computer. The accident forced me to be honest with myself for taking on too much. Where did this need come from, and what was I trying to prove?

What was interesting about it was the release the brave conversation with myself gave me. I had been given intense medication—morphine and valium—and I couldn't get rid of the neck pain. But the next morning, after examining my intentions, I was finally able to turn my head. That was the bravest conversation.

On Meeting Henry McClendon
and Restoring Brokenness

Some people come to restorative practices because something inside them has been broken and yearns for healing.

I came to restorative practices because my belief in the ultimate goodness of people, the stability of vital governmental institutions, and democracy as a means to redress historical and racial injustice was utterly shattered. Exhausted and out of options, I exiled myself to the Mexican jungle.

But life doesn't work that way. Life doesn't allow us to wallow in tacos and tequila when we have deep work. That's why I knew the only answer to Ted's request to go to Detroit to interview and shadow Henry McClendon for a week to write a series of stories was "yes."

Restoring Detroit

Henry is a humble man who dreams and acts audaciously. A Detroit native, Henry is a pastor of Berean Chapel and now the Director of Community Engagement for IIRP. He was formerly an executive assistant to Coleman A. Young, Sr., Detroit's controversial first black mayor.

Henry also served as the Southeast Michigan area director for Prison Fellowship Ministries, director of youth development for New Detroit Inc., program officer for the Skillman Foundation, and a former U.S. Army Reserve officer. He is also a husband and father.

"Restorative means bringing something back to its original intent," Henry said. "It means helping family be a real family, helping communities resolve problems, repairing harm, and strengthening relationships."

Henry heard about IIRP in 2008 and urged the organization to visit Detroit after the shooting of a public-school student. Since then, he has used training to pollinate restorative practices in Detroit's public schools, police departments, social services, health agencies, and even in the court system. His ultimate goal is to transform Detroit, once known for its crime, violence, and poverty, into America's first "Restorative City."

"A 'Restorative Detroit' looks like people valuing others regardless of race, age, or economic status," Henry said as I interviewed him in the food court of a local mall.

"Young people respect senior citizens. Older adults value children as treasures instead of trouble. People are looking out for each other."

Meeting Mrs. Washington

When you ask Henry how and why he came to restorative practices, he will likely tell you three stories.

The first is about a sheriff who bragged during a restorative justice conference that the practices were so ingrained in the local culture that they rented jail space to nearby counties. The second story is about how a restorative justice conference helped reconcile his father's relationship with two youths he previously mentored, who had attempted to rob and kill him.

Finally, the third story is about Mrs. Washington.

Henry met Washington in 1999 while working for a Detroit prison ministry and attending a restorative justice conference in Virginia. At the conference, Mrs. Washington talked about forgiving the man who had murdered her daughter, the grief of which led to the subsequent suicides of her son and husband within six years. She even allowed the man to live with her after his release.

"If restorative practices can create an environment where a mother can 'adopt' the man who murdered her son, I want to know how to do that," Henry said.

"After hearing her story, I committed to God that I would learn more about restorative practices," he continued. "The work will be complete for me when the sheriff of Wayne County can call neighboring counties and ask if they need jail space."

I realized restorative practices weren't just about healing our relationship with institutions and the people who have harmed us. Restorative practices are also about healing the fractured relationship among ourselves and each other. We must come from a restorative place within ourselves before that healing can occur in the world.

"People live in quiet desperation," Henry said. "They are in a room full of people and still feel alone. That desperation sometimes ends in gunfire. How do we turn (inner and outer) conflict into something healthy?"

Creating a Restorative Culture

Henry bristles against attempts to relegate restorative practices as a set of tactics and strategies to manipulate a specific outcome.

"It's not an event," he explains. "It's a culture. It becomes part of what people do regarding how we engage in work, respond to citizens, and parenting. It is intentional."

I witnessed the ripple effects of creating a restorative culture, not just a community, while shadowing Henry for a week. He shepherded me to charter schools, the Third Circuit Court, the University of Michigan-Dearborn, and social sector organizations. I met ordinary people who were taking the extraordinary step of changing the culture of their communities without government guidance or intervention. Because of Henry's integrity, compassion, and commitment to restorative practices, everyone welcomed us.

Ultimately, I believe Henry will achieve his vision of Detroit as a "Restorative City." He will succeed not because he wants to fix what is broken. Instead, Henry will succeed because he comes to restorative practices as a whole person and lights the path for us to do the same.

9

What We Can Do

Restorative communities are needed now more than ever.

Our world seems broken. Western democracies are heaving under the weight of political division, cultural wars, fluctuating economies, and the ripple effects of an ongoing global pandemic. We need more ways to create healing spaces that provide effective models for participatory decision-making, conflict resolution, and a sense of belonging.

But how? Public trust in institutions such as government, media, and healthcare has steadily declined over the past decade as political tribalism has overwhelmed the need to care for the common good. Whenever I suggest using a citizens' assembly to study and make policy decisions on critical issues, there is a nearly universal response: "What? You want me to trust that guy? I don't even trust people when I'm driving. How am I supposed to trust them to make important decisions that will affect my family and community?"

The answer lies in Mahatma Gandhi's famous quote, "If you want to change the world, start with yourself." Our world seems broken. But we are not.

Knowledge Is Power

Building a restorative community starts with a restorative mindset, as Govert van Ginkel reminds us. First, you must observe your thought patterns and beliefs. What actions are they generating? Are your dominant thoughts and behaviors reinforcing your fears or inspiring compassion, understanding, and joy? How can you change your thoughts and behaviors to create more connection, peace, and joy in your life if it's the former? These are brave and necessary conversations, as Keisha Allen would say.

Choosing to walk a restorative path is deeply humbling. Most people come to restorative practices because they want to fix something in their immediate environment. A nurse longs to foster collaboration and cooperation among colleagues to improve patient care. A charter school vice principal longs to decrease suspensions or expulsions.

Perhaps, like Commander Ewing, a veteran police chief aims to transform the nature of community policing and foster public trust. Investing in relationships through restorative practices unlocks something within us and our restorative path shifts. You realize the relationship that needs the most care and attention is the one with yourself. From a relaxed stance of grace and compassion, you care less about building and more about serving the restorative community.

It also helps to be a lifelong learner. I include a list of the top five books to read to help you build and sustain a restorative community in the Resources section of this book.

If you haven't already, I encourage you to sign up for a webinar, class, or course at the International Institute for Restorative Practices (IIRP). Based in Bethlehem, Pennsylvania, IIRP is a leading, global institution solely devoted to examining, promoting, teaching, and developing restorative practices. The school's faculty and staff are dedicated to effecting "real change within communities by strengthening relationships and fostering mutual regard among individuals."

IIRP offers instruction ranging from free webinars to professional development to a Master of Science Degree. Webinar topics include "Self-Care and Nurturing During Troubled Times," "Building Community for Consulting Partnerships," and "Processing Trauma Using the Relational Care Model." In addition, there are professional development classes for educators, social workers, coaches, and community leaders. Graduate courses are also available for those who want to deepen their understanding of restorative practices research.

Keisha Allen also offers restorative practices training through the Black Family Development Training Institute (BFDI) based in Detroit. The Institute aims to "strengthen and sustain homes, schools, and communities through professional development trainings that repair harm, restore relationships, and build civil societies." It provides training on the fundamentals of restorative practices, such as using circles effectively and facilitating a Restorative Justice Conference.

The Institute's four-week course, "Transforming Your Climate and Culture," answers a critical need in the restorative practices field. The course helps participants "learn how to align, engage, and effectively implement restorative practices within their setting."

Bridging the Gap

Being on the path of restorative practices might seem lonely sometimes.

Your supervisor thinks circles are a waste of time. Your teenager or spouse resists family circles. Your town council refuses to invest public money in restorative practices training for its police department. What do you do? How do you bridge the gap between the training you received and the restorative community you want to create?

Here are a few suggestions and reminders to help you along the way:

Gather with like-minded folks. Never underestimate the power of community. Sharing your frustrations and triumphs in a safe space opens the potential to learn from others, vent when necessary, and brainstorm new possibilities.

Building a New Reality hosts events led by Ted and Josh Wachtel on topics like citizens' assemblies, restorative communities, deliberative democracy, and sortition. The sessions typically include a presentation and small-group fellowship. Sign up on their website for their occasional emails to get more information.

Democracy Without Elections is a member-run nonprofit that promotes using democratic lotteries. Their website, democracywithoutelections.org, lists several affinity groups in the U.S. and globally interested in sortition and citizens' assemblies.

Finally, you can gather with fellow participants in online classes and workshops. Ask your instructors if they can steer you to existing groups. Also, check Facebook for affinity groups. There is something for everyone.

Invest in small experiments. It's great to take courses, read books, and gather with like-minded souls. But there comes a time to act. Start small.

For example, Adam Cronkright started by changing how student elections were run in a high school in Bolivia. "We Have the Choice" grew from restorative circles held in Kristin Verellen's living room after the 2015 terrorist attacks in Belgium. You can host a weekly check-in with your family, neighbors, or coworkers.

Some experiments, such as the mock citizens' assembly, will come with a cost. Apply for community and special interest grants to fund your project. You can also charge a modest fee to cover operational costs.

Develop a framework to guide your experiments so that they don't dissolve into "just another meeting." For example, before participating in a mock citizens' assembly, we met to decide its scope. We also met after the experience to discuss whether it met certain benchmarks.

A community circle can meet for a limited period and address a specific issue like reducing community gun violence or establishing a food program for kids during summer months. Or you can call the community relations department of your local police to see if they have any programs or events.

Share your progress. For better or worse, we live in a time when we have unprecedented access to other people's lives. If folks post photos of their daily outfits, pets, and meals, why not share photos of your restorative community event? Take a screenshot of participants from an online event (with their permission). Post inspiring quotes that help you along your journey. Start a monthly or even an occasional newsletter to send updates.

Sometimes we are reluctant to start a venture because we fear negative feedback that may never come. On the other hand, sharing your progress may encourage someone to join your project or start one of their own. We never know who we inspire by just showing up.

Change takes time. Dr. Martin Luther King Jr. said, "the arc of the moral universe is long, but it bends towards justice." More than a decade passed between Henry McClendon meeting Mrs. Washington and the implementation of restorative practices in nearly every sector of Detroit. You will experience peaks and valleys during your restorative journey. Remember that it's all good and all part of the process.

10

Afterword

Restorative Practices Hit the Streets

Ted had a singular idea when he approached me in 2018 to document restorative communities in the field.

He envisioned global tours where people could visit restorative practices "experiments" in Detroit and Kortrijk. Participants could spend time at Hope Academy, for example. They could observe a Community-Police Summit. Or they can learn about restorative communities while eating fresh produce grown on a restorative practices organic farm.

Visitors could learn what worked and what didn't. They could ask questions and engage in provocative conversations about how we wanted to live together as a society. Guests could form partnerships that could invest in one or more of the six facets of society.

COVID presented significant challenges to immediately realizing Ted's vision. However, we launched the Detroit Rising documentary series for audiences that were homebound, but still longing to see how restorative practices happened in classrooms, among court personnel, and nonprofit organizations.

I wrote *Restorative Communities: From Conflict to Conversation* to connect the dynamic research shared during global conferences and the families who were struggling to raise children in a discordant world. I wanted readers to see there is an elegant beauty in simple, but effective acts. Along the way, I met extraordinary people like Alice Thompson. Ms. Thompson is a civic leader and advocate for children and families in Detroit. She boiled the essence of a restorative community to having a key ingredient—a restorative heart.

"A restorative heart," Ms. Thompson says, "is a caring heart. It's a heart that believes and trusts in other people. It is a heart that listens. It's a heart that communicates. A restorative heart says, 'working together, we can make a difference.'"

Resources

Five More Books to Get You Started

Restorative Communities: From Conflict to Conversation was written as part of the Building a New Reality (BANR) library. BANR is a "revolution by conversation, advocating democracy in everyday life. It is "a non-partisan, evidence-based social movement that addresses the six facets of society's needs." We provide "both a roadmap to see where we are and a framework for participatory learning, decision-making, and action." How do we do that?

We read a lot, listen a lot, and put our ideas to work in the form of real-world experiments to test our theories. We also highlight the work of others who share our core values.

I offer five books to help you build a new reality in that spirit. In addition, I recommend some books written by BANR Founder Ted Wachtel and others in education and business that have shaped our thinking. So, we've got you covered, whether you want to explore our concepts further or are looking for thought-provoking books.

True Representation: How Citizens' Assemblies and Sortition Will Save Democracy by Ted Wachtel feels written for these times.

Citizens worldwide are now questioning whether centuries-old democracies will adequately address the urgent issues of a global pandemic, climate change, technology, political unrest, and racial justice. But unfortunately, what has worked for a racial and economic oligarchy isn't working for the rest of us.

True Representation explores sortition as a means of "bringing about true democratic representation in governance for all citizens."
Reinventing Organizations by Frederic Laloux is considered by many to be "the most influential management book of this decade." Laloux wrote the book in three parts. The first takes a historical look at organizational models and challenges us to imagine a "radically more productive" one. Part 2 uses real-life case studies from businesses, nonprofits, schools, and hospitals to illuminate the book's themes. The concluding part assesses the necessary conditions to create a new organizational model. It asks whether it's possible to transform existing organizations, and what results are possible after the transition.

Learning is Natural, School is Optional: The North Star Approach to Offering Teens a Head Start on Life by Kenneth Danford asks a question that most children have asked: "Do I have to go to school?" Danford and colleague Joshua Hornick left their public school teaching jobs in 1996 to find a better path. Part memoir and part how-to, the book explains how Danford founded North Star, a self-directed learning program for teens. With adequate support from parents and peers, "teens can learn and succeed without high school and its mandatory attendance, tests, and grades."

Swarmwise: The Tactical Manual to Changing the World by Rick Falkvinge "is a leadership handbook that outlines how the Swedish Pirate Party was able to beat the political competition on less than one percent of their budget. It also shows how any cash-and time-strapped executive or manager can use swarm methodologies, whether the goal is business, social or political."

The book covers everything from giving instructions to a marketing assistant to communicating on television, a hands-on approach to organizational change. Swarmwise is a bit aggressive in tone (such as "dropkick" the competition and its overemphasis on cost-efficiency.) However, its tips on project management ("plans must be tangible, credible, inclusive and epic") and choosing the right metrics have applications in various fields and endeavors.

Beyond the Schoolhouse: Learning for a New Reality by Ted Wachtel was "an angry young teacher's response to the ineffectiveness and injustice of traditional schools as he experienced them. Spiraling costs, declining academic standards, and shocking violence" are just as real now as when Wachtel wrote about them 40 years ago.

A new edition of the book is available, including Amazon Europe. We think you'll find Wachtel's advocacy for creating learning systems that provide more real-world, hands-on opportunities increasingly relevant, as parents seek alternatives to traditional learning models in the age of COVID.

About the Author

Winner of the New York Times Award for Outstanding Journalism, Kerra Bolton has explored how communities navigate growth and change for 25 years.

As a journalist, she captured the impact of U.S. immigration on small Mexican towns, a hospital in rural South Africa dealing with an AIDS crisis post-apartheid, and the rebuilding of a Honduran village after a hurricane ravaged the region. She also served on an investigative reporting team that uncovered systemic abuse in North Carolina's juvenile prisons.

Kerra currently spends her time in the Mexican Caribbean, where she is learning to swim, dive, and map sunken slave ships.

Building a New Reality is a non-partisan, evidence-based social movement dedicated to the decentralization of power and to participatory decision-making in every facet of society: learning, governance, care, justice, enterprise and spirit.

We advocate for more voice and more choice, in exchange for taking more responsibility.

Visit our website and look around. You can subscribe at the bottom of any page to get blogposts and updates.

Join us.

Revolution by Conversation

Made in the USA
Middletown, DE
03 April 2023

27841040R00096